EBURY PRESS

HOW NOT TO BE A SUPERWOMAN

Nilanjana Bhowmick has been a journalist for more than two decades, having won three international awards for her reports on gender and development. She began her career as a producer for the BBC Asian Network in Birmingham and The World Today, the flagship current affairs programme of the BBC World Service Radio based in London. She was the correspondent for *TIME* magazine's South Asia bureau in New Delhi. She has written for the *Washington Post*, Al Jazeera and *National Geographic*. Her non-fiction work, poetry and short stories have appeared in several international anthologies. Her book, *Lies Our Mothers Told Us: The Indian Woman's Burden* (2022), is a bestseller and has been nominated for several literary awards.

ADVANCE PRAISE FOR THE BOOK

'A definitive guide that will help every woman understand the unspoken burdens placed upon her by patriarchy and [how] to reclaim herself from them. Interspersing anecdotes with statistics and facts, you'll find yourself nodding in agreement all through it'—Kiran Manral, author of *Rising: 30 Women Who Changed India*

'*How Not to Be a Superwoman* is a fascinating read about internalized patriarchy that is extremely accessible and relatable as it navigates through everyday situations. It's not only important for women, but I feel very strongly that all young adults should read it, especially at an age when they can question what they have internalized and change it. Patriarchy has to be dismantled by men and women together, as it not only tries to maintain control over a woman's mind and body but also reduces men to designated roles and restricts them from exploring their inner diversity'—Onir, film-maker and author of *I Am Onir and I am Gay*

HOW NOT TO BE A SUPERWOMAN

A HANDBOOK FOR WOMEN
TO SURVIVE THE PATRIARCHY

NILANJANA BHOWMICK

EBURY
PRESS
An imprint of Penguin Random House

EBURY PRESS

USA | Canada | UK | Ireland | Australia
New Zealand | India | South Africa | China | Singapore

Ebury Press is part of the Penguin Random House group of companies
whose addresses can be found at global.penguinrandomhouse.com

Published by Penguin Random House India Pvt. Ltd
4th Floor, Capital Tower 1, MG Road,
Gurugram 122 002, Haryana, India

Penguin
Random House
India

First published in Ebury Press by Penguin Random House India 2024

10 9 8 7 6 5 4 3 2 1

ISBN 9780143464181

Typeset in Sabon by Manipal Technologies Limited, Manipal
Printed at Gopsons Papers Pvt. Ltd., Noida.

www.penguin.co.in

FSC
www.fsc.org
MIX
Paper from
responsible sources
FSC® C191020

To all members of the
'no more a superwoman' club

Contents

Introduction

> 'Of all creatures that can feel and think, we, women, are the worst treated things alive.'
>
> —Euripides, *Medea*

Dear family,

I am not planning that New Year's get-together this year so you can all collectively scream 'Happy New Year 2023', even as I am drooping in the background out of exhaustion. My feet hurt and I can sense a migraine coming on. I cannot fully comprehend or explain the exhaustion, but all I can say is that it is not completely physical. Something in my brain seems to just shut off towards the end of such evenings and then I am just an automaton—a robot if you may—programmed to smile, make small talk, serve and host.

My mind fills up with static—sometimes I have to ask people to repeat what they had said because there is a buzz in my ears and no other thought in my mind than to kick off my shoes, flop into bed and stay there in my pyjamas for three straight days. Remember the book *The Woman Who Went to Bed for a Year* by Sue Townsend?[1] I kind of feel that way. Trudging my way through life—tired and exhausted, a year in bed sounds delicious.

No, no, I know you don't mean to dump all this work on me—you are just conditioned not to see the labour that makes the machinery of our life run so smoothly. And yes, I do also know you don't care if I throw that get-together or not, but I am my worst enemy because I care about failing some unwritten rule of being a woman if I don't mark every festival or occasion with a huge dinner or lunch or something. But you know what? It would be nice if you could persuade me otherwise once in a while. I mean, I don't want you thinking: *ooh Mom didn't throw me a themed birthday party this year. What a big fail!*

Even though I know you won't be thinking on those lines, knowing it is never enough; between a mother and a child, a woman and her family, lies an invisible handbook—the handbook of patriarchy. It is invisible to everyone but us, the women, and even though we have been trying harder and harder to burn that book, it's a time-consuming process—a generational process.

I remember the way my friends used to look at me during lunch break when I would carry the same lunch every day—toast and an egg—the best my mother, with her 'double shift' of domestic as well as office work, could cobble together, while their mothers would pack sumptuous lunches. I had no problem with that lunch or with other things our society singled out to shame my mother (unconsciously or consciously) for 'failing' her role as a caregiver. I was always inspired by my mother's grit and determination to not give up her job even when the going got really tough (and the going was always very tough for her). The same cannot be said for a majority of women in this country who do not have a choice to change the status quo; the only choice they have is to give up what they fought hard to win—be it their jobs or their individuality—to retain the status quo.

Anyway, I digress as usual . . . so, yes, even though I love having my friends over, the cognitive and emotional burden of trying to take care of everyone is debilitating and doesn't allow me to enjoy the way I do when I am at a friend's house. But then at their house, too, I recognize the same exhaustion and hyper-alertness in them, and I know they are far from relaxed. It is extremely hard to wean women off carrying this burden.

Do you know how tiring the mental and cognitive load that comes with being a caregiver is? Taking care of others is not my superpower (there's a reason I don't have that cape). I might make it look easy, but it actually requires a lot of planning, organizing and problem-solving. It involves anticipating the needs of those you care for, thinking ahead to prevent potential problems (such as calling or messaging to find out about food allergies, or if someone is a vegetarian or a vegan—and while these might seem trivial to you, they do stack up to long hours of phone calls or messaging), and juggling multiple tasks at once. There are just too many moments of self-doubt, guilt and worry that can be difficult to manage. Sometimes it feels like I am carrying the weight of everyone's problems on my shoulders, and it's hard to find a moment of peace. So, I am trying to learn to say no and unlearn the expectations of doing it all and having it all that society has heaped on me and every other woman.

I know I bailed on the Christmas dinner and the Diwali soirée too. I chose me over everything else and I know you will be happy to know that I am happy—and if you are not, well then, it's time for all of us to unlearn the inequalities we grow up with and learn new ways to be equal, starting at home and then taking it out and about.

We have grown up with the indelible images of our mothers slaving in the kitchen, cooking and baking, gathering family and friends together and nurturing them—all with beatific smiles on their faces. But are their smiles really beautiful or have we been socialized to just see the smile and not the weariness underneath? Haven't we all hastily stowed away memories of those awkward flashes of our mothers, when they thought no one was looking and let that smile be replaced with an expression of exhaustion and weariness? Mothers are not supposed to be tired, are they? They are superwomen. And when they are tired, what do we do with it? How do we support them? We have never really delved deep into that, have we? But here's the fact—the soirées our mothers threw or we throw now, we scarcely enjoy. We are stressed and bogged down by the internalization that we must not let our hair down, that we are in charge of ensuring everything goes well and that everyone is looked after and fed.

It is no secret that women globally spend two to ten times more time on unpaid care work than men. This peaks throughout the year during festivities—annual, planned or impromptu. Like all unpaid caregiving, festivities are also imposed on women across the world. In India (specifically Bengal), the popular saying goes—*baro mashe, tero parbon* or thirteen festivals spread across the twelve months of a year. And during all these festivals, it's the women who are basting that turkey or chicken in the oven, it's the women who are making the curries and sweets in the kitchen or preparing the *sehri* and the *iftar*.* Even when there are no festivals, it's the women who are planning birthday parties and anniversary galas all year round. Don't get me started on the mad rush it takes to get back home to try and make you all fresh dinner or at least be present for it, and listen to your day or help with homework; or the craziness of trying to find fresh and organic ingredients to make you kiddos home-made everything from scratch—from croissant to lemon butter sauce to sushi. I didn't even know what crown I was vying

---

* The meal consumed before sunrise is called sehri and the meal consumed after sunset is called iftar.

for—for you were perfectly content with instant pasta and store-bought croissants. But as a working mother, I needed to be out there—ahead of anybody who could accuse me of not feeding my only child properly. What if I was to blame for the fact that you are a picky eater or that you have been underweight throughout your life? But, of course, I must be to blame for it—I am in charge of your development and nutrition—who else would the world blame but a working mother who is distracted by her career to take proper care of her children or husband? Phew—just thinking about it makes me exhausted. Hand me that anti-anxiety pill—because I am going to be curling up in bed with my book and a glass of wine. Don't dare to wake me up before it's January.

Lovingly yours,
Ex-superwoman-mom/wife/person/human

* * *

I woke up in a still-dark room—parched. I drank some water and fumbled for my phone—it was 5 a.m. Last night's get-together had gone on for long and I had merely had a couple of hours of sleep. And yet, here I was, up at 5 a.m. I could still sleep for another couple of hours, but I was wide awake and mentally listing out all the to-dos set for the day. Sleep was impossible, I realized after a while. I was too wound up about the day. The permutations and combinations going on in my mind to rearrange the day put my brain in overdrive:

Okay, if I say yes to this interview at 11 a.m., then it will give me the chance to quickly cook a special breakfast for my son because I feel so guilty about the party going on till so late last night and not being able to check if he ate properly.

Must plan my day so I am able to take my dogs for their daily walks.

It's the same—with little variations—every day, over the years.

Must plan my day so that I am done by the time my son comes home from school so I can spend some time with him and listen to him nattering on about his day—his little triumphs and tribulations.

Must wake up by 5 a.m. to be a functional worker+mum.

Where's the coffee? Oh no! I have run out of decaf!

Did I forget to order rice?

Did I thank the guests at the last get-together for turning up?

I have five days to file this story—and five hours a day to line up the interviews.

How am I writing two books this year? When did that happen?

My mind turns like a hamster wheel throughout the day. I cannot chill, I cannot take it easy.

* * *

I turned forty and something turned in my life.

And not just in my life—it seemed like my closest friends also crossed the bridge of striving to have it all and do it all, be the best worker, the best mother, the best daughters-in-law/daughter, the best friend, and reached the other side called *don't care, won't care. Don't want to be a superwoman any more.*

In the last few years, I have learnt to prioritize my work without feeling guilty about it. I stopped trying to be perfect at all times and learnt that there was no bravery in killing myself trying to do it all and do it perfectly. Women don't need to be perfect—they just need to relax and cut themselves some slack. In fact, a lot of slack.

I do not try to make everyone's lives easier at all points of time any more either—waking them up on time, reminding them of appointments or other stuff. My family has also found other ways of not missing appointments or caring for themselves without looking at me for interventions. I realized that they were always ready—I just needed to stand firm and stop trying to be a superwoman. I don't love them any less—neither do they, me. In fact, they are happy to see me watching a film or curled up with a book in my me-time.

Several other women were still slaving away at having it all—their struggle invisible and just a backdrop to our daily lives. But then came the biggest watershed ever—a once-in-a-hundred-years pandemic that brought with it lockdowns across the world. The result? Suddenly, women's unpaid caregiving burden was visible. Exhausted even more than before, women started speaking up about the burden of caregiving as well as the emotional and cognitive labour that is dumped on them, all in the name of nurturing and caring being a woman's superpower.

What is cognitive labour?

The anticipatory care that only women seem to be able to provide is their cognitive labour. A study defined cognitive labour as 'anticipating needs, identifying options for filling them, making decisions, and monitoring progress'.[2] Not just invisible but also taxing, cognitive labour was found to be largely carried out by women. Many men might want to be stay-at-home dads, but they rarely dabble in cognitive or emotional labour. Stay-at-home mums, on the other hand, don't just provide physical caregiving but also carry the burden of the family's cognitive and emotional labour. Working mothers, even with a stay-at-home spouse or a full-time caregiver, are only relieved of some of the round-the-clock caregiving of the children.

Also, the amount of time a stay-at-home father puts into caregiving differs from the amount put into caregiving by working mothers. In 2017, the Australian Institute of Family Studies[3] found that stay-at-home fathers 'dedicated an average of nineteen hours to childcare per week, compared to twenty-one hours for working moms on top of the thirty-five hours per week they were already spending at the office'.[4] The report also found that working dads spent only thirteen hours each on housework and childcare as compared to stay-at-home moms, who spent thirty-eight hours on both per week.

Covid-19 was a game changer. It imposed double or triple the caregiving duties on women—and the dam just burst. Managing the psychological and physical trauma of the pandemic along with the load of back-breaking caregiving was the straw that broke the camel's back.

After we all started working from home during the pandemic, I messaged a friend to find out how she was doing. When she didn't reply for many hours, I panicked and asked her if everything was okay.

'I just sat down after the whole day. I have been cleaning. The drain got blocked. Had to call the apartment block plumber and get it unblocked. Haven't eaten a morsel since morning. Need to cook dinner now,' she told me.

Another friend twisted her ligament. While we were talking, I told her, 'At least now you will get some rest. Make use of this.'

'What rest?' she quipped. 'I will still have to hobble around and clean. Otherwise, the house will get messy and no one else will clean it.'

The next day, I ran into her buying vegetables. The day after that, she was at the chemist's buying medicines for the pain in her foot. And yet, she was not able to do the one thing that would have ensured the healing of her foot—rest.

Cognitive labour is crucial in building and sustaining relationships, but it is also supervisory in nature. So even when women might have help with childcare or housework, they are still not free from cognitive labour because they are still planning and organizing in the background.

Emotional labour is, of course, anything that has to do with managing emotions and feelings. Caring for or worrying about the well-being of the family. Even as I am writing this chapter, I am thinking about Sunday lunch and while typing out the words, I have already ordered the chicken and some other groceries because well, that's what we do. I have no shame in admitting that while I have freed myself of all kinds of superwoman syndrome, I continuously slip back into it—like today, when both my partner and son are sleeping, and my housekeeper is on leave, I decided not to wake them up and instead, get as much done as is possible. *Oh! There's the doorbell—the chicken has been delivered.* There have been times when I have had bad meltdowns, and my husband and son would scurry to do the dishes or dry the clothes—but I shouldn't have to ask for help. Isn't that the whole point? If I don't ask and lay in bed the whole day, they are absolutely happy to glide along ordering food, making a mess and taking their time cleaning it. This is why I have started to ask them directly now, instead of hoping that they would see the mess and clean up.

The chicken has been marinated and is cooking in the stove. The kitchen is clean and sparkling, and I have just added another 1000 words to this draft.

I have understood that men are kind of slow in anticipating the needs of the people around them—this happens due to socialization. They are so used to their needs being anticipated and met by their mothers or wives that they have let their emotional intelligence lie in disuse. And this is where women have the edge.

Men or patriarchy have historically depicted women as feeble because they fear that if women fully realize their potential and demand equitable access to resources, the traditional notions of masculinity will be debunked. This is because true strength and informed decision-making are derived from both the intellectual quotient (IQ), which measures problem-solving ability, logical reasoning, and the capacity to comprehend and communicate complex concepts, and the emotional quotient (EQ), which measures the ability to identify and manage emotions, both in oneself and others. While IQ is gender-neutral, men have typically relegated EQ to the realm of women, unwittingly ceding to them significant power. Consequently, women tend to outperform men at work and in leadership roles (or would if they didn't have the double burden of caregiving, for which career often takes a back seat), owing to their superior combined IQ and EQ. In an article in *Forbes* magazine, LaRae Quy writes[5] that as an FBI counter-intelligence agent, she relied heavily upon emotional intelligence because while 'loud, boisterous and pushy behaviour' grabbed people's attention, it did not get any respect. However, emotional intelligence is subtle and often goes unnoticed. But it is what makes someone sharp and smart.

I observe people very keenly as human behaviour fascinates me. I have noticed that people who are loud, aggressive, pushy or rude are often extremely unsure of who they are and where their strengths lie. An emotionally intelligent person is someone who is completely secure in their capabilities—they know who they are and they quietly go around pursuing their goals.

'I have never had a loud voice but I've always had a strong one,' Quy wrote in her *Forbes* article. And that's it, isn't it? We need to own our emotional intelligence as it is what makes the world go round. Crucial in the age of artificial intelligence (AI), it enables us to navigate the human aspects of work, ethics and interactions that technology cannot ever replicate.

It is time to rethink how our homes, countries and the world function on outdated notions of leadership that corner women as 'soft' and 'weak'. And it is for us to change all these set definitions—and only more and more women in leadership and decision-making processes can enable that change.

And there's an economic benefit, too. Studies have consistently found that companies with more women in leadership positions tend to perform better financially. A report by McKinsey & Company[6] in 2020 found that companies with diverse executive teams were 36 per cent more likely to have above-average profitability. Credit Suisse, in 2019, said that companies with at least one woman on their board of directors outperformed all-male boards by 26 per cent in terms of share price performance over a six-year period.[7]

Secondly, women leaders have been found to possess certain traits that are highly valued in leadership roles, such as empathy, communication skills and a collaborative leadership style. Zenger Folkman, in 2019, found that women were rated higher than men in twelve of the sixteen competencies that make for an exceptional leader, including taking initiative, displaying integrity and honesty, and investing in the development of their team members.[8]

Finally, women leaders also manage crises better due to their feelings of empathy. According to the *Harvard Business Review*, countries led by women had significantly fewer Covid-19 deaths than countries led by men.[9]

It has been proved often enough that women possess superior emotional intelligence, but often enough, it has also been dismissed as a feminine skill and hence not desirable or needed in men. However, emotional intelligence is the true superpower of women—it is not merely something that makes us better nurturers or caregivers but something that also makes us empathetic workers and leaders. The reason women are expected to be superwomen is that they are conditioned to believe that their emotional intelligence is not a workplace skill and that they have to retain it for their caregiving roles while also learning the skills that men have specified as necessary to be leaders. Let me tell you a secret—undervaluing emotional intelligence often puts men at a disadvantage, especially as more women gain education and enter the workforce. These women are increasingly highlighting and challenging the patriarchal structures that have historically shaped and controlled their lives. If men don't harness their emotional intelligence soon as more and more spaces become gender-responsive, they will be left struggling to catch up. Future leaders are going to be compassionate and empathetic and yet strong and resilient—and a majority of them will be women. As Gemma Hartley, in her article 'Women Aren't Nags—We're Just Fed Up' (turned into a book called *Fed Up*.) says, 'Men just don't get it.' She narrates how she wanted a bathroom cleaning service as a gift for Mother's Day once, but her husband volunteered to clean the bathrooms himself, expecting a pat on the back, while she was left to pick up the mess he left behind. She went about cleaning the house, including putting away a gift box, without glancing at his handiwork in the bathrooms.

'In his mind, he was doing the thing I had most wanted—giving me sparkling bathrooms without having to do it myself. Which is why he was frustrated when I ungratefully passed by, not looking at his handiwork as I put away his shoes, shirt and socks that had been left on the floor. I stumbled over the box of gift wrap he had pulled off a high shelf two days earlier and left in the centre of our closet,' she writes, adding that her husband told her that he would have put it away if only she had asked—and yet, the box had been in the way for two days and he had been sidestepping it. How many of you just exclaimed in agreement here? I sure did. Hartley then explained to her husband 'the concept of emotional labour' that made her the manager of the household and how thankless a job it was. While Hartley's husband was blithely ignoring the box, she could not tear her eyes away from it in the two days she was pretending not to notice it. 'The whole explanation took a lot of restraint,' she wrote.[10] Reading this, I am nodding so much that I think my head may fall off. I see you too nodding or sighing vigorously at this point. It is actually pretty amazing the things women are not able to ignore that men are completely unmoved by—especially emotional labour. And emotional labour is so hard to track—I mean how do we really track the hours that are spent going over mental to-do lists, the minutes of panic over some imagined miss, the agonizing hours when you are away for work? A woman's mind is never at rest—it's a machine that is at work 24/7/365. How do we quantify that labour? One way is to use time use surveys (TUSs)* and quantify it with the help of leisure time. TUSs have found that on an average, men have forty-nine minutes more leisure time than women. But even when women are purportedly at leisure, are they really unwinding? For example, when I am eating my meals, I am also reading or watching something on television because I cannot fit all three in separate time slots. The days I cook, I do so in between my writing—again I do not have the luxury of taking out separate time slots for either. Every woman I know is multitasking at all points of time—not because they are good at it or it's something only women are good at but because how else are they going to fit in everything that is expected of them in a given day? Studies have shown how women predominantly plan household activities and also do 'mental work' at home—things like creating grocery lists or calling the handymen, reminding children of their engagements, etc. Emotional labour, simply put, is putting other people first.[11]

* Time use surveys measure the participation of men, women and other groups in paid and unpaid activities.

While many women like me have somewhat successfully made caregiving a shared responsibility of every family member, we still struggle to share cognitive or emotional labour mostly because its nature is so vague. The popular perception is that women do these things effortlessly, but that is not true at all. Women are socialized to believe that being able to shoulder these loads makes them valuable in society and their families or communities. This is why they do not think twice before helping out at the local temple making food for hundreds of people or organizing family get-togethers—even if it means they have scant enjoyment and are exhausted with all the hosting, cooking, making sure everyone is happy, that they ate and drank and had a good time, while just wanting to plop on the bed and sleep.

Take, for example, Christmas. In 1990, a study found that 'while Christmas shopping may be a "labour of love" to some, it is most widely construed to be "women's work"'. It is still counted as 'women's work' today.[12] Almost three decades later, women are still more stressed about Christmas than men.[13]

If women say no, they are deemed to be selfish. So, they take on all the caregiving, including the mental and cognitive load of taking care of the family, taking care of anyone in need, sick friends and relatives, and lending empathy to those who need it. But it has a debilitating effect on their mental well-being—it should hence come as no surprise that women are nearly twice as likely as men to be diagnosed with depression, as a report by the World Health Organization found.[14] An article in the *Lancet* titled 'Gender differences in the association between unpaid labour and mental health in employed adults: a systematic review' suggests that unpaid labour, which is disproportionately shouldered by women, is an under-researched topic. It carried out a search of six databases and examined the association between different forms of unpaid labour and mental health and found that 'inequities in the division of unpaid labour expose women to greater risk of poorer mental health than men'.[15]

A major cause of depression among women is chronic stress. 'Women are more likely than men to say they feel stressed out. Although individual women have different stressors, many women cite work overload, life circumstances or abuse as their main source of stress,' says an article by Mindset on 'Why Women Are More Prone to Depression'. 'Many women work full-time and still manage to shoulder most of the responsibility at home, including taking care of young children and/or older parents. Women are also more likely than men to live in poverty, be single parents and suffer some form of abuse (sexual or physical), all of which can contribute to the development of (and help perpetuate) a major depressive disorder.'[16]

According to a report by the American Psychological Association, women experience stress-related health problems such as headaches and sleep disturbances more often than men.[17] And it won't be too much of a stretch to say that this stems from the pressure to be a 'superwoman' at all points in time. I cannot imagine a time when I haven't suffered from migraines; I often feel like I was born with this as an inherent condition. On the other hand, I have never, in our nineteen years together, come across my partner complaining of a headache. The amount of painkillers I consume on a weekly basis is enough to sustain a small pharmacy for sure. Recently, I suffered a migraine attack with a pain level of 500+ on a scale of 1–10. (Yes, it was that bad!) And yes, I have learnt to live with migraines and headaches and all sorts of inexplicable aches and pains, but this one was at an unimaginable level. I had to be hospitalized and injected with pain medication through a drip for the medicines to work and the headache to subside. The brain scan came back clear. The doctor said it was stress. As I sat there listening to him, I felt everything getting blurred out for a moment and all I could think was that stress landed me in hospital with a drip on my hand. It was a moment of sudden epiphany—I write about women's mental health and the effect of stress and unpaid caregiving on women's lives, and here was another reminder of why it is so important to keep shouting about how unpaid caregiving and the superwoman syndrome affect the quality of women's lives. Because women's pain is often invisible and dismissed as being imagined. I have had enough doctors tell me over the years that I would be a great case study for all the symptoms I report that have no explanations. Oh well, then do better as doctors, I guess.

The idea of being a superwoman is also deeply intertwined with the concept of perfectionism, which research has shown can have a negative effect on mental health. Studies on perfectionism have found a correlation with higher levels of anxiety, depression and stress.[18]

Depression also looks different in men and women. A Johns Hopkins article titled 'Depression: His Versus Hers' says, women are more likely to embody the symptoms of depression in dissatisfaction 'with their body image and have guilt, feelings of failure, difficulty concentrating and sadness'. Older women are 'more likely to experience stress, sadness and sleep problems when they're depressed'.[19]

I, too, for long, thought it incomprehensible that if we were to have guests over, I wouldn't cook for them. Or that I would let festivals pass without marking them by cooking up a storm for friends and family. For a long time, I just couldn't look at myself in the mirror or in pictures. I was even absent from most family holiday pictures. I also experienced imposter syndrome and was always furtively watching my back, lest someone took away all my hard-won achievements. Because who was I, if not a superwoman who was as diligently managing her home as work?

Women have been socialized from a young age to understand that their larger role in a family is that of a caregiver—that they are the only ones able to care for and nurture. For example, have you ever wondered why women care so much about cleaning up a mess as compared to men?

Men may be immune to mess because they have internalized the gendered nature of housework and believe that someone (their mother, wife, sister or domestic help) will clean up after them, but women do not operate in the same way. Once, I was visiting a friend's house and saw her rushing around packing for a work trip while also stressing about how dirty the kitchen was. Her stay-at-home partner had cooked and fed the kids but had not cleaned the kitchen. As we talked, he relaxed on the couch engrossed in his phone and she said, 'The kitchen has been a mess for hours—I can't leave the home in such a mess. If someone walks in, they will blame me for being careless and untidy.'

Women often face situations where they feel worried about being judged. They are especially concerned about not being good enough at providing care, something many people think is a key part of being a woman. They are anxious about being judged or feeling like they are not doing enough or being enough if they do not keep a perfect house, attend parent–teacher meets at the school, organize playdates for their children, bake for the school bake sale and so on and so forth. This fear of being judged hangs heavy on stay-at-home and working mothers alike.

Studies have shown that women are judged more harshly for a less-than-perfect home than men. A study titled 'Good Housekeeping, Great Expectations: Gender and Housework Norms' found that men and women were 'differentially held accountable for housework'. 'Women with relatively tidy rooms are judged as less clean, less moral, less likely to be viewed positively by visitors and less comfortable with visitors than men with tidy rooms,' the study found, adding that this was in part because of 'the greater moral criticism and social consequences women are expected to encounter'.[20]

This is why even when women go out to study or work, we still feel the need to come back home and help others in the kitchen or take care of our siblings, get the homework done, plan for the next day and so on and so forth.

Women need to openly discuss the burden of being unpaid caregivers, a role that often involves a lot of thinking and emotional work and leads to stress and mental health challenges. It's important for them to let go of trying to do everything perfectly and instead, focus on finding a more balanced way of living. It is time to accept that **no one has it all** and that making a choice is not a bad thing. Once we accept this, then only can we influence policy and laws to reflect this choice in terms of paid parental leave, flexible work arrangements, equal pay or even a caregiving allowance for stay-at-home parents.

The superwoman myth, apart from its individual toll, also has broader societal implications. When women have to choose between caregiving and a career, they are expected to choose the former, not just in our country but worldwide. This means that women are still not able to participate in the economy at the same rate as men. Research on gender parity has found that if women participated in the economy at the same rate as men, the global gross domestic product (GDP) could increase by $28 trillion by 2025.[21] And why are women not participating in the economy as much as they should? Because the caregiving expectations our society dumps on them don't leave much time for personal growth. We want women to be superwomen, to be supermoms and also career divas. Unfortunately, they are all mutually exclusive, which is why there is an urgent need to debunk four myths that have made women slaves to the superwoman syndrome. Hopefully, debunking these myths will help women explore their potential as equal human beings.

What Are These Myths?

1. *Women are better at caring*

No, sir. Caring is not a gift of the vagina. This is just another stereotype. A study published in the *Journal of Applied Gerontology* in 2018 found that there were no significant differences in the caregiving experiences of men and women and that both genders reported similar levels of satisfaction with their caregiving role.[22]

When it comes to paid caregivers, there are more women than men in this field globally. According to the data from the International Labour Organization, women account for 67 per cent of health and care workers globally but earn, on average, 24 per cent less than male workers. Much of this gap is unexplained but possibly exists due to discrimination against women.[23]

For instance, the nursing agency from where we hired my father's attendants paid their female attendants (who live with the family) Rs 10,000 per month while male attendants were paid Rs 12,000 for eight hours.

But here's the thing: Both his male and female attendants were equally competent. I thought about why the women were paid less than the men—possibly because when women work as caregivers, it's looked upon as an extension of their role at home and not a skill, but when men work in caregiving, it is a skill. As we know, women are not born with special caregiving genes. If you socialize men from a young age about caregiving, they can be good caregivers too. They do a great job when they get paid for it, don't they?

2. *Women are better cooks*

Cooking is a life skill like no other—human beings have to survive to work and in order to work, they must be properly nourished. When the Industrial Revolution happened (1760–1840), it was decided that it was men who were more suited to work in the factories, doing the heavy lifting, etc., and women were relegated to being the nurturers. Luckily, this is not the eighteenth century any more and we have come a long way from those gender stereotypes.[24] Today, women are also vying for traditionally male-dominated jobs in factories and elsewhere. So, isn't it time to bust this myth? Cooking is a life skill. You do it enough times, you are exposed to it enough times and you learn. There is no significant difference in the ability of men and women to cook, and there are numerous examples of male chefs who are just as skilled and accomplished as their female counterparts.

Do men and women have different cooking styles? Generally speaking, yes. Often, women have been raised to be good at household tasks, which include cooking and cleaning. So, while everyone has their own unique way of cooking, shaped by personal tastes and social influences, these differences don't really affect how much we enjoy cooking or the dishes we make. There are typical ways men and women approach cooking—men might show off a bit more and take pride in their cooking, while women might be quietly confident since cooking is often a routine task for them.

Take my family, for example. My dad was an amazing, almost showy cook. He loved learning and making new dishes, especially on Sundays. I can still picture him in an apron, ladle in hand, and a cigarette hanging from his lips, totally in his element. But my mom was the behind-the-scenes hero—prepping, chopping, and cleaning up after Dad's cooking adventures. She used to joke about preferring her simple meals since Dad's fancy ones meant a lot more clean-up for her.

At the end of the day, cooking is a basic skill everyone should know, and that includes cleaning up afterwards. So when we teach our boys to cook, let's make sure they learn to tidy up too. It's all part of the process.

And if women were better cooks than men, then we wouldn't have so many talented male chefs who have achieved global recognition for their culinary skills. Jamie Oliver from the UK and Vikas Khanna, Ranveer Brar and Sanjeev Kapoor from India, are just a few examples of male chefs who have received numerous awards and accolades for their innovative and outstanding cuisine.

Now, here's a contradiction: While it's a universally held belief that women are better cooks, the culinary industry has historically been dominated by men, and there have been significant barriers for women to enter and succeed in this field. Because women are only good as home cooks or home chefs, right?

3. *Women have more patience*

Women have as much or less patience than men. There have been various studies conducted on gender differences in patience and their findings are inconclusive as to whether one gender has more patience than the other. A study published in the *Journal of Economic Psychology* in 2010 found that men and women had similar levels of patience in a delay discounting task,* which measures the ability to delay gratification.[25] A study titled 'Gender Differences in Time Preferences' published in 2014 found that women were more patient than men in certain situations, such as waiting for a larger reward, but that there were no overall differences. Gender is just one of many factors that can influence an individual's level of patience.[26]

* Delay discounting task is a psychological test used to study an individual's preference for smaller immediate rewards versus larger delayed rewards. This task is often used in research to understand decision-making processes, particularly in the context of self-control and impulsivity.

4. *Women can multitask*

Women can multitask. As can men.

The belief that women are inherently better at multitasking is a common stereotype, but it is not supported by evidence from recent studies and reports.

In fact, several studies have found that multitasking can be detrimental to productivity and cognitive performance regardless of gender. For example, a 2019 study, 'Multicosts of Multitasking', found that multitasking, or trying to do several things at once, actually makes our brains work much harder than we might think. When we multitask, our brain isn't really doing everything at once. Instead, it's quickly switching back and forth between different tasks. This constant switching is tough on the parts of our brain that help us focus and manage what we're doing. While our brains try to keep up with all this switching, multitasking often means we don't do any of the tasks as well as we could if we focused on them one at a time. So, even though it might feel like we're getting more done, multitasking can actually make things harder and less efficient.[27]

Moreover, a recent study published in *BMC Psychology*, 'Are women better than men at multitasking?' found that there were no significant gender differences when it came to multitasking abilities.[28]

While it is true that women may have more experience juggling multiple responsibilities, such as work and caregiving, it does not necessarily mean they are better multitaskers. In fact, research has shown that attempting to multitask can lead to increased stress and decreased well-being, which can have negative impacts on both men and women.[29]

Do you know what stay-at-home mothers do all the time? They multitask. But, for women, multitasking is not just about juggling home and kids—it is about juggling physical, emotional and cognitive labour. And if men want to be more present, they must be more present not just for their children but also for their spouses. Multitasking is not rocket science and it's definitely not a feminine superpower—at its core, it is about time management. While an overwhelming majority of people believe that women are better at multitasking because of their experience in managing children and other household work, 'women and men perform equally when required to switch attention between tasks or perform two tasks simultaneously, according to a new study. The finding adds to a growing literature that contradicts the widely held belief that women multitask better than men'.[30]

5. *This is all 'women's work'*

There is one bigger myth that looms over all these myths—that all of the above is 'women's work' and men are not good at them. We are in 2024, where equality should no longer be a hard concept to grasp. Yes, men are socialized to treat caregiving and housework as 'feminine jobs', but they also will have to catch up on their emotional intelligence if they want to stay in the game. This means sharing caregiving in its entirety—because while caregiving is not the only criterion to develop emotional intelligence, it certainly contributes to it.

In today's world of social media and information overload, it should not be difficult for women to unlearn biases and learn to value themselves more.

At a recent talk at IIM Ahmedabad, I asked a room full of students if they envisioned a future where their wives worked and, together, they sustained a healthy, happy and prosperous lifestyle. The answer was a firm yes. But when I asked if they also envisioned a future where both contributed equally to caregiving—including sharing the cognitive and emotional load—there were a few nods amid what was mostly an unsure silence. The answer was right there in the uneasy silence in that room. Even if they couldn't explain the discomfort they were feeling, it had already taken hold—men can unlearn the socialization that they are not good at housekeeping if women can unlearn the belief that they cannot be breadwinners. It is high time men realize the superpower of emotional intelligence.

Unlearn that a wife is not another pair of hands to help a mother with housework, or if you live alone, to clean and cook for you.

Lend a hand at home. Learn to recognize the signs of overwork in your partner. If she's harried, irritable, always tired and quieter than usual, it should not take much to understand that she is overworked. Often, she herself wouldn't understand that she is overworked. Tell her she is overworked. Try and help her. Don't sweep it under the carpet as 'women's problems' or hormones.

What my friends and I have learnt over the years—what we remind each other constantly:

It is okay to say no.
It is okay to insist on your own wants.
Sacrifice is a trap.
Asking for help is a great start.
No one is perfect, women don't need to be either.
Burning the toast or rice is not a failure—it is just being human.
Emotional intelligence doesn't make us weak—in fact, it is our superpower and if we can use it in our personal lives, we can definitely use it in our professional lives to get ahead.
And most importantly, be mindful of emotional and cognitive labour.

Honestly, if I had a daughter, I would teach her how not to be a superwoman.

I would tell her burnt toast is okay. That you can scrape it and slather it with butter and honey and still enjoy it. Yes, it will taste a bit burnt. A bit bitter. But you can live with it. No one can have it all. No one should want to have it all. Perfection is an illusion, a rabbit hole.

As women, we've been conditioned to believe that we can do it all. We're expected to be the perfect partners, mothers, employees and friends, while still maintaining our sanity and self-care. We strive to be the ultimate superwomen, taking on more than we can handle and sacrificing our own needs for the sake of others. But what if I told you that being a superwoman isn't all it's cracked up to be? What if I told you that it's time to shed the cape and embrace a new, more balanced way of living? The goal of this book is to empower women to reject the superwoman myth and embrace a more holistic, balanced approach to life. By prioritizing their own well-being and setting realistic expectations for themselves, women can achieve greater fulfilment and happiness, both in their personal lives and in their careers.

The idea of 'having it all' has long been held as the ultimate goal for women. The myth of the perfect work-life balance, where women can excel in their careers while also raising a family and maintaining a thriving personal life, is an ideal that many women strive for. But seriously, junk that goal. There is no one way to look after your family—earning for them and giving them a better life is also a form of caring. And no matter how much you try to balance your life and career, you will never be satisfied. So be *you*, be human and do what is humanly possible.

From the time women began to take on the role of co-breadwinners, they have been pulled between family and work—something that feeds the superwoman syndrome constantly. This dilemma manifests mostly as mommy guilt—most women I know, including myself, are constantly battling with the fear that they are not doing enough for their children or not really present for their children or that any development issues that arise may be because of their neglect, even when they are literally killing themselves to balance caregiving while also substantiating the family income. Way back in 2009,[31] a Pew Research Center study on American working moms found that women felt the 'tug of the family much more acutely than working fathers' and that 'family appears to be one of the key reasons that many do not break through the "glass ceiling" to the top ranks of management'. I have made those choices myself—and I still do. Before taking on any assignment, long-term or short-term, my most important consideration has always been the duration I would have to stay away from home.

The reality is that achieving a perfect work-life balance is often an unattainable ideal, particularly for women who face additional barriers and challenges. Instead of striving for the myth of having it all, it is important to prioritize what matters the most to us as individuals.

Do men have it all? Maybe, but only because they have a different definition of having it all—one that includes family and work but prioritizes their role as workers more than caregivers. On the other hand, women's definition of having it all is something that they did not come up with by themselves and were conditioned to accept, even if it meant that they prioritized their roles as caregivers and treated the worker part as negotiable. So, if they felt strongly about 'having it all', they could kill themselves trying or could give up. Either way, it's a definition created to benefit men. Superman saves the world—superwomen juggle domestic chores and work responsibilities. Do you see what I mean?

It's time to call out this immensely sexist concept of having it all and redefine it. Let having it all mean that we prioritize ourselves, are kinder to ourselves, allow ourselves rest and leisure, and do what makes us happy—be it work, family or both. But the choice has to be ours and it has to be informed—not a sexist mirage that we run after without questioning its need in our lives.

The Covid-19 pandemic was bad news in too many ways—we still do not fully know how much damage it has done even in the bodies of survivors. But it also shone a light on women's struggle to balance their lives and the inhumane expectations they had to feel the pressure of. It also left us with the feeling of 'now or never'. It *really* is now or never. I would rather it be now, wouldn't you?

I do not care about being a domestic goddess any more. Making croissants from scratch? Nah! Too much work. Planning get-togethers every month with thirty to forty people? Yawn! Long live potluck.

What other issues are modern women in India and elsewhere struggling with in a world that is created by and for men? The list is long and varied, but some of these issues are the imposter syndrome, the superwoman or having-it-all syndrome, what I call 'the perfection trap', various forms of relationship guilt (the most common among them being mother guilt), gender stereotyping at home and at work, low self-worth, a lack of leisure or communities where they can talk and share and not feel so alone.

When I started writing this book, I already had a set of women in mind to interview. However, on a whim, I posted a request on social media asking women who were trying to negotiate the various struggles of being a woman to get in touch with me. My inbox exploded. There were so many women who wrote to me over the next two days that I was completely overwhelmed. But what struck me were the messages that said 'Your Twitter thread is so heart-warming—we thought we were the only ones.' It is sad that while we have undoubtedly come a long way, women still feel alone in their experiences, and that patriarchy has created such a trust deficit among women that they are unable to talk to each other with complete honesty. For instance, patriarchy has taught us to never malign our families—no matter how abusive they are—and we still live our lives bound by these rules, even with our friends. Even when we find ourselves in our tribe, somewhere we are still holding back. The dilemma is not in the telling but in the not telling. The Twitter (now X) thread completely took me by surprise and here I was, suddenly in the midst of what seemed to be a growing community of women willing to share their experiences—the good, bad and the ugly—with other women. I hope that this book will not just be a reference point for women to live their best lives but also one that will bring women together, encourage them to share their experiences and build communities.

I hope that these stories of women who have been able to escape the expectations and perfection trap will help many more to find their way out of the maze that is the not-so-fabulous lives of modern women in India and elsewhere.

1

The Enlightenment: What Women Want

> 'I always did something I was a little not ready to do. I think that's how you grow. When there's that moment of 'Wow, I'm not really sure I can do this,' and you push through those moments, that's when you have a breakthrough.'
>
> —Marissa Mayer

The day I went blind was a dull day. It was a patchy, unremarkable April evening when suddenly, the lights dimmed and the world went into deep shadows. Just like that. Without the stealthy steps of an illness or accident.

I was on my way to see a friend. I was sitting in the car, with temperatures threatening to climb over 45 degrees outside. The air conditioning in my car had given up the pretence of cooling. The car right in front was emitting black smoke in a thin spiral as Delhi's bumper-to-bumper traffic refused to budge.

The buzz of the daily, local market grew around me with the swirling crowds. The noise dipped and picked up as I surrendered to the heat-induced inertia. The steering wheels were sweating out the smug heat and the incessant, impatient honking. There was an article in the magazine that I never finished reading.

Snippets of a Bollywood song floating in from an auto rickshaw with a garish pink interior. The driver was lip-syncing to the song: '*Gulabi aankhen jo teri dekhi* . . .'

The rest of the evening was a whirlwind of medical ERs, medicines and the depressing smell of hospital corridors echoing with the whispers of nurses.

An adverse reaction to a migraine medicine had triggered a glaucoma attack. The world in front of my eyes was hazy and dark. My first reaction to this blindness was complete shock. Those two weeks lasted an eternity.

After the first couple of days of shock, however, I was surprised at the keenness with which I was hearing and feeling.

Who knew the dogs barked so madly at passing cars? Or that the ceiling fan in my room was so noisy? Or who knew my car made its own music while travelling on gravel? And who knew birds sang and fought so much in the concrete jungle of the Indian capital! I have never had the time to stop and listen.

And more than anything else the relief at not having to stay on top of everything was palpable. I didn't bother with the menu or groceries. I did not bother with work. I was not working toward a deadline for the first time in my life. There was no niggling sense of fear or failure or self-doubt. I was in a good space. A great space. All I needed was to see again.

And who knew the house could run without me trying to control everything? Food got cooked, was eaten, groceries were ordered, fees were paid, the child reached his school, sat for his exams, the husband made it to work, managed to pay his bills and stay alive and not die of hunger.

When I was learning to swim, my trainer once took me to the deep end and told me to just walk into the water. I looked at him incredulously.

'I will drown,' I squeaked.

He said, 'No you won't. Just have faith and walk in.'

I did. As I went down into the pool standing and hitting the water, the fear left me. I was not worried any more about drowning or not being able to breathe. I was weightless and fearless in the vacuum of water around me.

When I rose to the surface again, I took a deep breath. I didn't want to do it again but I knew if I had to, I would. And come back up again.

Both these events turned out to be the beginning of an age of personal enlightenment for me. When you are forced to drop the ball—you stop and think hard and then you decide that you need to turn your life back—that it really is *now or never*.

* * *

During the Age of Enlightenment between the seventeenth and eighteenth centuries, an intellectual movement emphasizing reason, science, and individual rights, challenging traditional authority and promoting ideals of liberty, equality and secularism that greatly influenced political, philosophical, and social thought across Europe and beyond—women's role in society had come under the scanner. It was during this time that women in western Europe found creative ways to rise above the circumstances that placed them firmly in the domestic sphere. The concept of salons—a social and intellectual gathering of people who would meet at the house of a well-known or intellectually inspirational person to discuss the latest cultural trends, from literature to politics, from art to philosophy—became a vehicle of women's enlightenment. And as the salon took place in the home, it allowed women to participate and contribute.

At the time, Mary Wollstonecraft, a British author and activist, in her influential work, *A Vindication of the Rights of Woman (1792)*, had warned that if women did not reject 'the soft phrases, susceptibility of heart, delicacy of sentiment, and refinement of taste' and acquired strength of body and mind, they would become objects of pity and contempt.[1]

In India, a century or so later, feminist activists like Savitribai Phule were raising the war cry: 'Awake, arise and educate. Smash traditions - Liberate!' In one of her poems, there is a complete understanding of what the world only started talking about post-Covid-19—a woman's unpaid burden of care and how she has to disproportionately shoulder that burden. 'The woman from dawn to dusk doth labour/The man lives off her toil, the freeloader,' she writes. 'Even birds and beasts labour together, Should these idlers still be called humans?'[2]

* * *

Priya's father had always been her greatest support. While she never told him about her abusive marriage—it was his constant support that helped her deal with it. She was still trying to keep everything together, keep up the appearance of her happiness, when he fell severely ill—an illness from which he would never recover. His death brought a pause in Priya's life.

'I was stuck in an abusive relationship for fifteen years; I had accepted the abuse for long but things changed in 2010,' the fifty-three-year-old engineer says. What happened in 2010? Her father suffered a heart attack that he couldn't fully recover from. 'His condition deteriorated and he was in the hospital for two weeks. During this time, my husband would not allow me to visit him. He would say "You go to work, let your sister go and visit him,"' Priya remembers. But her sisters live abroad and her husband's argument that she should prioritize her work was because he was unemployed at the time. 'He was always in between jobs,' Priya says. 'And even though at work I was told to take it easy, to take as much time off as I needed, he wouldn't let me. I realized then that this relationship was not worth it.'

'It's not like we didn't have money—we had enough and yet, he wouldn't let me spend any of it on my father,' she says. 'And then my father died, and I was done with him. I did not want to keep working at it. Not any more.'

We have come a long way—yet, we are still figuring out the various inequalities women face in their daily lives. We still expect women to cater to stereotypes, quietly ignore instances of discrimination and bow down to patriarchy at all points in time.

But there's a quiet revolution underway too—an age of enlightenment that women from all over the world are experiencing, it is a personal journey of renaissance, reform and enlightenment.

It's a moment of reckoning when we stop and take stock of our lives—when we suddenly make time to hear the sounds of nature, when we take a moment to breathe and empty our minds of stress and anxiety and the constant spool of things to do. This moment could come in our twenties or thirties or forties or later—but it comes for sure. The moment when we start questioning things rather than accepting them at face value is the time when our entire life kind of unspools and we realize that of the million minutes that seem to comprise our day, we don't get many for ourselves. How do we clock this moment though? Because the change in our lives comes from clocking this moment that I call the 'epiphany moment' of a woman's life cycle.

This phase, however, is not a universally defined or recognized stage like adolescence or middle age.

Certain periods or transitions in a woman's life are often associated with self-discovery, personal growth and increased self-awareness. These moments can be considered to be 'enlightenment phases' for some women. It is extremely important for women to understand and identify when they happen so that they do not get dismissed as 'just a phase'. Very often, when women are at this stage, people surrounding them secretly dismiss the change and expect it to go away. On the other hand, women who have been able to identify and clock this stage have been able to unlock the secret of an equitable life.

One of these phases might come in young adulthood, which typically occurs in the late teens to early twenties when women are transitioning into adulthood. During this time, they may explore their identities, values and aspirations, which can lead to self-discovery and personal growth. During this critical time of transition, women may leave their family homes, pursue higher education, start their careers and form new relationships. This new-found independence and responsibility often lead to self-exploration, where women question their beliefs, values and life goals. They may experiment with different lifestyles and choices, seeking to understand their true selves and what brings them fulfilment. This phase can be both exciting and challenging as women navigate the complexities of adult life and work towards defining their identities.

Many women experience a significant period of reflection and self-evaluation during midlife, which is usually in their forties or fifties. This phase, often referred to as a midlife crisis or transition, can prompt women to question their priorities, re-evaluate their goals and seek a deeper sense of purpose. For men, this is a midlife crisis, but for women, it is midlife *freedom*. Isn't it beautiful? When most men are going through a crisis, women are actually finding themselves. Since their entire lives are filled with one crisis after another, they don't have the luxury of a midlife crisis. Instead, they are hurled headlong into a sudden epiphany about their lives, and none of it is very rosy.

In some women, major life events such as marriage, becoming a mother, divorce or the loss of a loved one can trigger introspection and lead to an enlightenment phase. These events may prompt women to examine their roles, relationships and values, leading them to personal growth and transformation.

For other women, this phase comes post-menopause. At the end of their reproductive years, they start to focus more on their personal growth and choose to pursue passions and interests they may have put on hold earlier.

Every woman experiences this phase—they might often not know how to deal with it or what to call it, but all of them feel its liberating force, either secretly or openly. Of course, each woman's journey of self-awareness and enlightenment is unique, and there is no predefined timeline for these transformations.

'I come across a lot of clients going through this crisis. The reason is simply that by the time you reach midlife, you have experienced enough, are more aware, and have enough wisdom to decipher that society has been bullshitting you. When you feel betrayed by society, you want to do justice to your original self. So, I help a lot of women going through this phase,' says Dr Priyanka Yadav, a psychiatrist and talk therapist based in Delhi NCR. Yadav begins by treating the symptoms that manifest in her clients the most, such as anxiety, depression, stress, eating disorders and weight issues, to name just a few. Yadav believes that it is super important for women to find a *unique* purpose in their lives. 'When we align our lives with that purpose, we tend to be happier. This process is particularly important for women, as they often face societal conditioning that limits their potential. You have to find your true meaning. In this process, you become more courageous and start listening to your own voice. This journey can bring about a lot of positivity and good energy, and it's a significant part of the healing process.' And it is only through self-reflection, openness and a willingness to embrace change that we can find deeper meaning and purpose throughout our lives. That is how I identified my purpose in life. After struggling for years to be all of everything every time, I realized that it was writing that brought me meaning and purpose in life and that there was no shame in prioritizing it over everything else. But like everything else in life, the process of enlightenment, too, is a journey. There is no timestamp as to when you might come across your 'eureka moment'—the moment when the rest of your life falls apart and you see it for what it was—a mirage. There is no timestamp for when you turn this corner and say 'enough—no more!'. But whenever that time comes in your life, don't ignore it. This is who you were always supposed to be. So, be that person.

There are many studies and articles online that will tell you how to identify this phase. I will tell you how I identified this phase in my own life. It all began with a deep distaste for catering to societal norms and expectations of me as a designated superwoman—the same norms and expectations I was socialized to shoulder with a smile. But I was having none of that bullshit any more. I felt like my third eye opened and I was seeing through all the bullshit that I have been fed by society through popular culture—through media, advertising, etc. Once you identify gender stereotypes and how social conditioning normalizes them in your life, you cannot unsee them again. I couldn't either. They flashed like a neon billboard in my head—spelling out in big, bold, bright letters exactly how they have limited me.

This might feel like a midlife crisis to many and yet it carries a meaning distinctly different from the conventional understanding of such a crisis. The term 'midlife crisis', when applied to men, is a kind of an easy-breezy term, thanks to how it's portrayed by popular culture. It is treated almost like a rite of passage. However, women's midlife crisis is a much deeper experience, one that is not talked about often—least of all by women themselves—and has remained something invisible, ignored. Ada Calhoun wrote in her article 'The New Midlife Crisis: Why (and How) It's Hitting Gen X Women', ' Part of the reason we don't know much about women's midlife experience is that the focus has often been on men. For them, the "midlife crisis" (a term coined by psychoanalyst Elliott Jacques in a 1965 journal article) usually involves busting stuff up—marriages, mostly—but also careers, norms and reputations. We all know the drill: panic comes on once a man starts losing his hair, and results in a frenzy to reclaim lost youth and unearth college vinyl. Recommended treatment: regular application of scantily clad younger women and brightly coloured motor vehicles.'[3]

If I were to describe my life to someone, I would say: I am in my mid-forties, I have had a successful journalism career, I have written for most of the world's top publications, I have worked with the best organizations, I have won awards for my writing, I have written a bestselling, award-winning book, I have an agent for my novel, and *yet* I wake up every morning feeling like I have achieved nothing with spiralling disappointment. Whenever I am asked to introduce myself, I don't know what to say, and when someone else is describing me, I am awestruck (sometimes even embarrassed)—it doesn't feel like the person being described is me. And I can pinpoint the period when that started happening to me—it was when I turned forty. I was tired of the constant rush to prove myself to myself and everyone else. I realized that, as a woman, I had always held myself to an impossible standard, which in turn led to such a severe burnout. I started questioning if I needed to push myself so hard if I really needed to over-give, overperform, over everything so much. I mean if the deadline is on Monday, then why do I need to send it on Sunday? It never mattered that I did those things—I was still paid less than my male colleagues, and I still had fewer career growth opportunities. So, I stopped. Not in one day but over a period of time. I am now in my late forties, and finally, I am able to turn a blind eye to mess; I can breeze past without getting worked up, I honour deadlines but I won't kill myself to deliver early, and most importantly, I have stopped hustling.

'We don't talk enough about women's health, let alone their mental health,' says Dr Yadav. 'For years, women's mental health issues have been dismissed as a phase or an irritant, including stereotypes such as *a woman will be irritable when she's going through menopause or during her periods.* The mental health aspect of it has always been ignored and that's why even women remain unaware that they need help navigating through the transitions of life,' she told me.

When we talk about midlife crisis, we are primarily focusing on changes in behaviour and the impact of hormones, rather than exploring how individuals contemplate their life journey. In my conversations with women, I have come away with the understanding that upon reaching mid-life, they find themselves to be more intelligent, insightful and possessing better judgment than they did in their youth. Is this simply a result of accumulated life experience or could it be related to the enhanced ability for pattern recognition observed in the midlife brain? If so, what role does this play?

Terri Apter, a psychologist who has been working on and with midlife women, says in an article in *Psychology Today*,[4] 'Women often describe a "filter" or "veil" or "judge" that comes between their thoughts and wishes on the one hand, and their decisions on the other. They can be about whether to buy or bake a cake for a school party, whether to agree to take a meeting at work even when it will result in overload and fatigue, whether to go on a vacation with a partner even when you really get no enjoyment from the skiing or dining that your partner enjoys so much. These decisions are often minor events, but they can shape one's daily life.' She also noticed a difference between the speeches of women in their early forties to those who were close to fifty. The difference was that while the former often referred to 'internalized or shadow voices, voices reminding them about norms of the caring woman', the latter consciously stopped their inner critics or didn't exhibit having one. The reason, she says, middle-aged women are more assertive, adventurous and willing to break the rules is because there is a change in 'how we process our thoughts and identify our feelings. There is less running interference from others' expectations and standards (real or imagined) as we reflect on what we want to do.'

Yes, both men and women struggle to balance their personal and professional lives, but historically, women have had less support in managing their personal and professional lives—mostly because of their caregiving duties which are non-negotiable in certain cultures, while in other more gender-equal societies, there are subtle expectations that women know and understand and cannot say no to. Even when I was studying in the UK for my masters, I would see women shouldering a majority of the care work and definitely all the mental load. From getting groceries to caring for the children to cooking—they did it all. Yes, the men sometimes helped out—for e.g. in doing the dishes. But they were always 'helping out' if you know what I mean? (Just like when women work, they are 'helping out' with the family finances). But care is a shared responsibility, and as women, we need to stop feeling overwhelmed when the partner shares it and retaliate by taking on even more physical or mental caregiving. There's no end to this vicious cycle till we end it in our minds. And a woman's real and much invisible load is the mental load they carry around with them like a halo or a cape. Occasionally cooking, cleaning or doing the dishes is not all of the caregiving—it goes way beyond that. For those men who are sincerely interested in building equal homes, I urge you to read up on caregiving—what it entails and why even in more gender-equal societies where men share household chores, women are burnt out and have had enough. Putting women on a pedestal as selfless and nurturing has only harmed them—if they leave the pedestal, they are bad and selfish, and if they stay on the pedestal, they are overworked and depressed. The 'good woman', 'good mother', 'good wife' and 'good daughter' pedestals have been created by patriarchy to keep women's desires in check.

Many women today are more aware of these societal pressures, and this awareness can trigger a conflict between their authentic selves and their conditioned selves shaped by society. This inner struggle can lead to feelings of rage but it also marks the beginning of their transformation.

Many women, in fact, feel uncontrolled rage or a lack of control over their lives at this stage, hating the powerlessness of their existence. This rage, Dr Yadav says, is often the first symptom of anxiety or depression. 'It's quite common to experience anxiety or depression during midlife, which can manifest as irritability. This irritability can lead to outbursts of anger due to a lower tolerance for frustration. When we dig deeper, we find that, by midlife, individuals often gain a clearer understanding of reality and begin to see through the societal expectations imposed on women.'

But also, by midlife, most women know the truth—that they must change or they will remain short-changed by life. It is also at this time that women are surer of themselves—they have lived long and they have lived hard lives, they have struggled and hustled and tried to be the best to everyone but themselves. But halfway through life, they look back and see that they have left themselves behind. There is no other option but to go back, pick themselves up and rebuild who they are.

'By the time most women hit midlife, their children are either teenagers or about to be. Parenting can be tricky during this time, especially given the influx of technology in our lives. It is now so much more complicated than before. Many women feel lost and unable to handle this change because most women, especially mothers, have less access to technology or no time to learn how to navigate it. Children are also often impatient when it comes to teaching their parents, especially their mothers, new technology. But this also has pushed many women to self-learn new skills, including technology and the internet,' says Aashi, a Delhi-based researcher in her early thirties, who identifies as a Bahujan queer. 'Most women by their midlife are disenchanted with the idea of the "eternal motherly love" and they are ready to put to the best use what is left in them and of them,' she adds.

If you trawl the internet, you will see that the mommy vloggers or daily routine vloggers are all women in their late forties and beyond who have taught themselves technology to keep up with their children perhaps, but it has now financially empowered them too. Many daily routine vloggers on YouTube have hundreds of thousands of followers, sponsor products and earn a respectable amount of money every month—all this along with a self-confidence boost, of course.

Aashi's mother bought herself a mobile phone only last year. Aashi takes time out to teach her how to use the phone, especially social media platforms, to stay in touch with her and her life. 'She is an ailing woman in her late forties who has to work due to the lower income situation of the household. However, she finds time to scroll through my Facebook timeline almost every day,' she adds.

Many women in their forties also suddenly find themselves purposeless as their children grow up and don't need round-the-clock care any more. Known as the empty nest syndrome, it affects women deeply.

'Women spend a lot of time nurturing their children and once their kids leave home, they just don't know what to do with their time. The nurturing gave them a purpose,' Dr Yadav says.

But, as the mother of a young adult, I feel this is also an invaluable opportunity to not just reassess our priorities and reclaim time and energy for ourselves, but also to reorient our dreams and aspirations that have been dumped unceremoniously underneath the muddy football boots, school uniforms, early morning matches, packed lunches, parent–teacher meetings, holiday homework, unrealistic 'mummy expectations' from schools, music or self-defence classes (or both), play dates and nutritious but tasty meals.

A homemaker and a mother of two in her late fifties says that it was hard in the beginning when she realized that her children didn't need her any more. 'I had built my entire life around their needs and wants, and suddenly they were their own people. They were taking their own decisions and very soon, they would be flying the nest,' she says. But after the initial realization of this sudden void, she also began to see what this really meant or could mean for her life and her own personal journey. 'I am also looking forward to this time—to do things that I never could before. Take up a hobby, travel solo or maybe paint. I never had any time to devote to my painting and I am excited that now I will have the time to paint, and who knows, maybe an exhibition or something—one can always, dream, right?' she laughs, adding 'I don't know if I should be saying this out loud though.'

Her hesitation is completely legitimate. A woman having the time to devote to herself is quite the anathema in our society. And for her to feel happy that she is now free of child-rearing duties is even more repugnant. It is completely at odds with the mother goddess image we impose on women once they become mothers—smilingly sacrificing their every desire and dream at the altar of their family's happiness. In the old days (not *that* old either), they were expected to turn to God. I know my mother was ridiculed enough for dealing with her empty nest syndrome by turning to read more books instead of devoting that part of the caregiving to God. My mother-in-law, the late Pranati Bhattacharya, too, was a carefree soul. A former professor of political science at a college in Kolkata, she was openly agnostic and took much delight in reading (and writing), pro bono teaching, attending theatre, accompanying my father-in-law, the late Nabarun Bhattacharya, and her mother-in-law, the late Mahasweta Devi (the two were the best of friends for most of their lives), to their readings and other engagements, and socializing with friends and acquaintances—it was pure joy to see her transform her empty nest syndrome into a wonderful period of self-discovery and self-pampering. I have always wished to grow old like her—with an abundance of grace and self-awareness. Hesitatingly perhaps, but the women of today are better at utilizing this time—in fact, they have better access to resources to utilize at this time than before. We live in an age where there is a proliferation of online courses and women's travel groups, and solo travelling is becoming more and more popular—and it is all because women are realizing the importance of 'me'. A majority of solo travellers across the world are women in their fifties.[5] A New York City-based luxury vacation booking platform conducted a study that showed that 68 per cent of solo travellers in 2017 were women. In 2018, the number rose to 73 per cent.[6] In India, too, the number of women solo travellers is rising. Reports suggest that more than half of all solo trips in India between 2014 and 2015 were undertaken by women travellers.[7] A 2018 study found that women wanted to travel solo to experience a 'life-changing moment', to 'experience freedom', and to 'escape the identity and roles' that society has imposed on them, and 'wanted to utilize their time in the trip to introspect their life. Solo travels have helped them to understand themselves more properly, giving them the opportunity to focus on their own well-being rather than others'.'[8]

As a field reporter for most of my life, who travelled solo almost every other week, I can confirm that solo travelling is life-changing for women. It helps in building perspective and confidence, and most importantly, allows you to be who you are. And at a very, very fundamental level, it allows you to order room service, which is my favourite thing to do when I am travelling solo! Heh! The fact that I had no role to play in making the food that I would be eating—even though I don't cook as much, I still have to plan the meals—and that it would be served to me, still delights me. But on a serious note—distance from the family helps women understand that if they can let go, their partner can also step in. And when they start stepping in, the exception starts becoming the new norm.

Aashi's mother used to be a poet before she was married. The pressures of marital life, especially after her daughter was born, meant that her pen dried out and was replaced with more practical preoccupations. 'Instead of writing poetry, my mother would discuss my educational expenditures with my father over the weekend,' she remembers. 'She still doesn't write but now that she has a phone, she reads other writers and often sends me inspirational quotes or writings.' But this is just the beginning; very soon, she will again put pen to paper and write a poem. 'Share that poem with me,' I say to Aashi.

I have been working with gender inequalities all my life, but it was not till I turned forty that I really started thinking about my life and how sharing my experiences could create a community; and how I could create a repository of lived experiences, and live and learn from them. As a writer, I wrote a book, *Lies Our Mothers Told Us*, a deeply honest take on my own struggles with the patriarchy-imposed double burden of paid work and unpaid caregiving as well as the harmful social conditioning that controls our every action. And the book created a community of women who came together to say, 'Us too'.

Now, women are coming up with innovative ways to empower other women and address various gender inequalities. We have realized that the best solutions for women will come from women, because of our shared experiences. Mridvika, a thirty-nine-year-old computer engineer, founded a tech start-up called Sama, which aims to help companies retain more women in the workforce. Sama uses a predictive modelling and diagnostic survey tool to examine six key areas—women's goals, relationships, health, infrastructure support, career development and workplace safety—and understand why women drop out of the workforce. So far, they have piloted their tool in a few IT services and financial services companies.

'The insights we've gained have revealed various reasons for women leaving their jobs, such as workplace culture and lack of gender-sensitive leadership. Our goal is to create gender-equitable workplaces and drive systemic changes to retain women in the workforce,' Mridvika says. 'However, we face challenges due to the lack of data and demonstrative evidence, making it difficult to drive policy changes effectively. I am passionate about making a meaningful difference in women's lives and helping organizations understand why women quit jobs, leading to impactful interventions and inclusive workplaces.'

And when did her moment of enlightenment come? In Mridvika's life, it took a significant life event—in fact, a series of significant life events—marriage and babies. 'Two years after my marriage and post two babies, I suddenly had this huge burden of caregiving on me,' she says. 'I didn't ask for help, because, you know, who does that? I needed to prove that I can manage it all, right? I did not want to ask for help because I thought asking for help would make me feel, you know, less competent. That I think was my moment of enlightenment. Knowing that I was not infallible.'

But it took her a while to act on this moment. 'I read a bunch of books which kind of flipped a switch in my head to say, "I don't need to do it all by myself." That I didn't need to wear a cape and say I'm a superhero. And then I started asking for help because unless a woman asks for help, no one sees her burden. So, yes, please ask for help.'

Mridvika's husband is a very progressive man but why would he want to be pushed out of his comfort zone unless there was a trigger? And that trigger would have to come from his partner. The pushback has to come from us. It's really as simple as asking for them to help in the kitchen or change the sheets in the rooms while the woman does other stuff. Make a routine and divide up the duties. Start early with children, especially the male children. When I was in the UK and we lived in a shared flat, I would see only the Indian male students grumble about the cleaning rota. This is not just about entitlement, but misinformed entitlement, and it is embarrassing. And it must be called out on a day-to-day basis. Don't push it down saying 'it doesn't matter' or that you have bigger battles to fight. *This is the battle. This is the fight. Stay and fight.*

Nidhi, a life coach born in Bilaspur, Chhattisgarh, and now based in Dubai, says she experienced a shift after she turned forty. 'You are suddenly invisible—I mean you are there, very much present, and yet, you feel completely unseen. You're still important to the life of the people who love you, care for you and vice versa, but they also kind of just stop seeing you.' That understanding was the epiphany moment for her. 'That's when I stopped trying to be what people wanted me to be.'

For one, Nidhi stopped colouring her hair. 'My hair was mostly grey and I coloured it like we are supposed to do but by that point in my life, I didn't care any more. I didn't want to look the part that society had decided for me.'

'I was exhausted by these trips to the parlour and then, I chose not to do it again. I am happy in a certain way. Initially, it was an identity crisis. When women came up to me and said that they wished they had the courage to embrace their greying hair too, I realized that it was not actually *that* hard to be the person you want to be. Nowadays, I am rarely affected by what people think of me. Been there, done that. Right now, what I think of myself is what matters the most.'

Other women have had their moments at different phases in their lives. 'I don't know if it was enlightenment or just survival instincts, but I moved out of my parents' house four years ago. I grew up in a really dysfunctional family so conflict is our default. Moving out has really helped me work on myself as the distance provided a lot of perspective,' a thirty-two-year-old media professional says.

Enlightenment means different things to different women. For some, it is about letting go; for some, it is about imbibing things that social conditioning taught them to stay away from; but for most, it is about turning a corner in their lives.

How have women identified this key moment in their lives and how have they benefitted from it? They have been able to walk out of abusive marriages and toxic parental relationships, and most importantly, set boundaries in relationships—both in their personal and professional lives. After living with disappointments, they have embraced the unknown. They have jumped in the deep end knowing that they will come out on the other side fine. It is not easy, but it is doable. It is the only fight that matters in their life.

For Natasha, this moment came to her in the form of a nervous breakdown when she was in her early twenties. 'It took a long time for the doctor to diagnose that it was not something physical. Since then, I have been conscious of drawing lines in my life and not taking on more than I can. However, at every stage in my life (newly working professional, young bride, new mother), it took a while to draw my boundaries. But I did.'

Something similar happened to Nasreen, too. 'It took me twenty-one years and my pre-teen daughter to push me to get out of a bad marriage, despite opposition from all sides. Getting my divorce was really liberating,' says the fifty-four-year-old lawyer. 'And despite all the mental, emotional and financial problems, I have to say that I feel more confident and comfortable in my skin now than ever before.'

When I was brainstorming this book, I went to X (formerly Twitter) to crowdsource experiences but also to understand how much interest was really there for this sharing of experiences—'best practices' in corporate lingo if I may. And I was surprised. While I had expected a lukewarm response at best, my tweet exploded. What was even more surprising was that women were directly messaging me, saying 'Your thread in itself has become a community. I look at the thread and I feel heartened that I am not the only one. There are other women dealing with this and maybe together we can teach each other what to do—how to negotiate this minefield that is a woman's life.' The second most important response was the idea of creating a repository of women's lived experiences—how they were dealing with the daily struggles of being a modern woman and more specifically, the double burden of being a modern woman. Some of the messages were from young women—students, who were confused as to why they felt compelled to reply to my tweet, definitely younger than the age group the tweet was targeted at (thirties and beyond). 'I was really confused because I am twenty-five years old, and I don't know why I replied to your tweet. Have I seen enough of life to share my experiences?' she says. 'But I wanted to share and that was a surprise because I hadn't really thought of my life in terms of "I have had enough."'

Other women say they were the happiest when they turned forty. 'The sense of freedom was overwhelming. It's not that I had achieved all my goals, dreams and aspirations, but I was extremely comfortable in my skin. I was completely at peace with who I was and where I was. I was happy with the way I was supporting other women and completely happy with who I was then. That was a major shift,' says Saloni Singh, a gynaecologist who has now found a new vocation as a life coach.

Many other women confirmed that they experienced their awakening—either by being let down by a close relative or just because they had had enough.

For a young academic, this moment came after her father let her down about a long-running dream. 'My father is a well-to-do businessman and we have a small plot of land on which I wanted to open a literary cafe. This is what I wanted to do for years. I was told I could, once I "proved myself worthy" which, for him, meant pursuing a PhD. I came back from Germany last year only to do this and once I arrived here, he shut down the whole project,' she says. 'That is when I realized that even if you do everything correctly and be the good girl, the despotic patriarch can still take everything away from you. So, what's the point anyway?'

'I stopped worrying about what others think about me over the last few years,' says another woman I spoke to. 'Now that I have let go of those standards, I live on my own terms and my boundaries are set. I feel happier and freer!'

And finally, the one nugget of wisdom that I would be personally carrying with me forever: *Feeling good comes with a lot of goodbyes.*

2

No Can Do: The Power of Saying No

'To end certain cycles in your life, you will need to say no to things you've once said yes to in the past.'

—Robin S. Baker

Priya learnt to say 'no' much later in her life, like most of us. And once she learnt it, there was no looking back. She started saying no to being unappreciated and unacknowledged, no to being taken for granted, no to her abusive marriage and her abusive parents-in-law. These *noes* led her down a path of liberation and gave her the courage to finally walk away from her abusive marriage.

That's the power of a no.

The smallest words in the English language are the most potent, the most emotional, the most gender equitable and yet, the hardest to utter.

No
Yes
I
Me
Self

Out of these words, the word women die a thousand deaths to utter is *No*.

If we say no, will we still be liked?
Will I be promoted?
Will I be acknowledged?
Will I not be isolated?
Will I be misunderstood?
Will I be enough?

No. Such a small word, but it has so much transformative power, especially in women's lives. But we have such a hard time saying it in our personal lives as well as professional. Why do women have such a hard time saying no? If I look at my life, I see a long list of noes disguised as yeses. The extra assignment at work that I knew would make me work through the night, the invitation to a get-together that I knew I would not enjoy, the invite to an interview or talk that I knew I couldn't fit into my schedule, and you want to know the funniest one? Committing to writing two books with deadlines that were two months apart. Why? You guessed it! I couldn't say no. And even as I am drowning with the workload of a full-time job and staying up nights over the weekend to get the books finished, all I can manage is a sheepish grin. *I have a problem saying no!* There were so many things I could have done—said no to that last-minute assignment dump at work, spaced out the books so that they wouldn't become such an inhuman task—in short, just learned to say no. Sometimes, I think of how when I would go to visit my grandmother-in-law, writer–activist Mahasweta Devi, a fiery and feisty woman in her personal life, at her home in Kolkata, often just before the Durga Pujas, I would see her with two notebooks open on either side of her at the writing table. She couldn't say no to many of the puja special magazine requests and would just write simultaneously. Was I inspired by that? Greatly. My late mother-in-law, a former political science professor, had so much trouble saying no that she would be on her feet throughout the day just running errands, helping someone with something, someone else with something else, and these activities could range from teaching to visiting older relatives to attending various social events, while also managing her work and her family. I never heard her say no to anyone till the day she died. And I could see how stressed and harried it made her—this inability to say no and trying to keep everyone happy. And that is why women can't say no—a deeply embedded fear of not being liked or making people unhappy. While no one told us that it was our duty to keep everyone happy, they did something worse—they socialized us to believe that this is our most important job. This is called social conditioning or the systematic training of individuals within a society to adopt specific thoughts, beliefs, emotions, desires, and reactions that align with the approved norms and values of that society or its various groups. 'Even for the most stalwart women, there comes a moment when our inner resolve fails us and one of the simplest sounds in the English language (n o) comes out as "OK", "sure", "why not", "all right", "I suppose", "if you really think so" or just as a sigh of resignation,' Suzanne Gerber wrote in her article titled 'Why Even Strong Women Sometimes Have a Hard Time Saying No' in 2012.[1]

And there is a good reason why we think a thousand times before we utter a definitive 'no', because saying no might appear simple, especially for men, but for women, it is loaded with apprehensions. It's a word that can upset the status quo and historically, women have had to pay a price for doing that. In a world where women are expected to follow rules and expectations, 'no' is a weapon, a vibe, a way of life—it contains within itself the power of consent, the power to transform a woman's life, boost her self-confidence and make her aware of her own worth. And that is exactly why we have been socialized and taught never to say no; because when women say no, they don't care any more and when they don't care, they cannot be suppressed so easily. Every 'no' is a strike against societal norms that decide who a woman is supposed to be and more importantly, who she shouldn't be. This inability to say no means that women have forever put themselves last, that they have accepted discrimination as a way of life, that they have accepted that doing it all and doing it alone is the price they have to pay for their empowerment, and sometimes to justify or hold onto their empowerment. At home, they have normalized being overworked as love and being underappreciated as life, and at work, they have normalized under-acknowledgement as a price they need to pay for prioritizing their role as caregivers.

She is damned if she does, and doubly damned if she doesn't.

In the rigmarole of providing caregiving to all and sundry, women forget to care about themselves, and in not saying no to the world, they keep saying no to themselves. Saying no is the first step to self-care and for most women, self-care is akin to a luxury or indulgence. Poet and essayist Audre Lord had written in her 1988 essay, 'A Burst of Light', soon after she was diagnosed with cancer for the second time: 'I had to examine, in my dreams as well as in my immune function tests, the devastating effects of overextension. Overextending myself is not stretching myself. I had to accept how difficult it is to monitor the difference. Necessary for me to cut down on sugar. Crucial. Physically. Psychically. Caring for myself is not self-indulgence, it is self-preservation, and that is an act of political warfare.'[2]

Self-care is merely taking back control of our lives from a culture that subverts women. It is about women's physical and mental well-being and hence, their basic human rights, and overturning a world that runs on the exploitation of their invisible labour and caregiving. Self-care is an important act of rebellion and it starts with saying no.

Research suggests that women may feel the need to prioritize the needs of others over their own, leading to difficulty in declining requests without feeling guilty or stressed about the consequences. Not being able to say no and not setting boundaries leads to increased stress and anxiety. Individuals who struggle with boundary-setting often report high levels of stress and anxiety.[3] American Psychological Association's Gender and Stress reports have consistently found that men and women react differently to stress. Their 2012 report found that women reported symptoms of stress as lying awake at night, overeating or eating junk food or completely skipping meals. They also reported other symptoms of stress such as 'feeling depressed or sad to experiencing headaches and changes in sleeping habits' or constant fatigue, anxiety, feeling overwhelmed, feeling exhausted, feeling like crying, or suffering from upset stomach or indigestion.[4]

All of these findings are so important even if they are not in the Indian context. For years, I have struggled to understand these symptoms in myself. Women I know, friends and acquaintances, struggle with it too. And yet, we push it under the carpet and carry on. We try to manage our stress but more often than not, we fail. I have failed spectacularly to manage my stress. If you eavesdrop on women's conversations, I can guarantee you that you will hear one phrase across the board—'I am so exhausted.'

According to the APA, while women were more likely to report physical symptoms as effects of stress, they were also better at devising stress management strategies. *Better at devising stress management strategies or shoving it all under the carpet?*

For the better part of my life, I thought I was successfully controlling my stress but I was merely devising ways to bypass it without addressing it because if I was really devising strategies, it would have started with saying no to unreasonable demands on my time, not just at home or work but to so many other people I know or barely know.

The APA report also found that women were much more likely than men to say that having a good relationship with their families is important to them, but fewer women say they are doing a good job at succeeding in this area; they are also more likely than men to say that having a good relationship with their friends is important to them, even though friendship is cited less often than family for both men and women; and nearly half of all women said they have lain awake at night in the past month because of stress.

Women are apparently also more likely than men to say that they lacked the willpower to make lifestyle and behavioural changes, and that they needed to be less fatigued and have more confidence in themselves to improve their willpower. And finally, interestingly, while most men would say they needed to earn more money, women said they needed to find more time. Yes, more time. Sometimes, I wish days had forty-eight hours instead of just twenty-four. Or that I could be less tired so I could make use of more of those hours, but since I have hit forty, I can barely stay up beyond 10 p.m. I have also had Covid-19 four times, after which I feel like exhaustion is the only constant in my life. And in a cruel twist of fate, I can't sleep beyond 4 a.m. because anxiety about losing hours of sleep is ever-present in my mind. If I could say 'no' more, I would probably have fewer demands on my time. And believe me, every day, I practice various ways of saying no—not hesitantly but determinedly, confidently and without guilt peppering my words. Just the other day, a woman acquaintance apologized to me for saying a 'blunt no'. They went on to explain that they had so much demand on their time that they were struggling to cope. I messaged them back saying 'I love a blunt no' and in that moment, we were united because we realized the power of saying no. I respected her more for saying a blunt no, but I also recognized the societal conditioning that makes us apologize for saying a blunt no. And since then I have said a few blunt noes of my own, it feels good. But the fact that I still struggle with saying no means that I am always burnt out—professionally and personally.

And while we might think that burnout is specifically a work-related problem, I believe that it is not. Women suffer personal as well as professional burnout that usually manifests in overwhelming exhaustion, feelings of cynicism and detachment from the job, and a sense of ineffectiveness and lack of accomplishment. Sound familiar? To me, it does, and I felt it keenly in both my personal and professional life. If a workplace is defined as any place where a person works, then that makes the home a woman's workplace too. Hence, would it be so illogical to assume that like we face burnout in the workplace, we face similar burnout in our homes too? When the two collide and combine for me, it sometimes manifests in physical illnesses, sometimes in an out-of-body feeling where I feel like I am merely following the motions of my life, and sometimes in just vacant thoughts. And of course, there is anger, resentment and depression.

As Paulo Coelho said, 'When you say "yes" to others, make sure you're not saying "no" to yourself.' A 2021 article, 'How Women Who Do It All Can Combat Burnout', examined how women who were used to doing it all could beat burnout by saying no. 'If you say "yes" more to others then you're saying "no" to yourself. Learn to re-evaluate your responsibilities and become OK with letting things go. If you're maxed out at work, then consciously let something else go,' the article had advised. 'At home, re-evaluate your to-do list and consider outsourcing some of the house tasks to your partner or hiring a service. Remember, "No" is a complete sentence in and of itself. You don't need to qualify your answer or give any rationale.'[5]

So, how did Priya start saying no?

After her marriage, Priya had mostly trodden the path of non-confrontation and compromise, but her patience broke when her husband and his parents began to prevent her from doing things for her own parents. Along with her enlightenment came the ability to say no, when her father died and she struggled to look after him or be with him in his last days.

'My former in-laws troubled me a lot. They were very traditional people who hosted a lot of festivities.

Despite having a full-time job, I would never say no to cooking for guests and hosting them. And yet, they would make me feel like I was not enough,' Priya remembers. 'But it came to a head when they began to prevent me from looking after my ailing father.'

Rebellion was simmering inside of her and she erupted immediately after her father's death. For Priya, her father was her everything; he was her biggest support, and when she lost him, she found herself with her back to the wall and the only way forward was to stand her ground. Her father was not there any longer to provide her emotional support and she felt bereft. 'I didn't really care any more.' She stopped talking to her abusive mother-in-law.

Losing a parent is hard and people, especially women, because so many of their decisions are based on not letting their parents down, find it to be a turning point in their lives. But sometimes, the loss of a parent could also make us feel lost and anchorless, and say yes to things that we should ideally say no to.

'I did not process my dad's death for the first seven years. I blocked it. It was a mistake. I just wanted to get on with my life, ignoring the trauma of losing my father. I was merely going through the motions because society expects you to be a certain way, so I was married by twenty-five and had my kid by twenty-nine. It was only later that it struck me that I had just lived life on the surface. If my dad hadn't died, I would have probably lived a different life,' says Dipsikha, a former entrepreneur turned health coach, who lost her father when she was only twenty-two.

The moment she realized that she had been saying yes to the wrong things in life, Dipsikha walked out of her marriage and moved to a different city with her daughter. She wanted to explore life like her dad would have—spontaneously. 'Maybe it was my way of dealing with the grief that I had put away for so long. I now want to live every day like I would have if my dad had not died when I was so young,' she says.

'I said yes for the wrong reasons and now, I say no for the right reasons,' she adds. 'A little older, a little wiser.'

Constantly saying yes can result in feelings of resentment and disconnection to our self. Psychologists have often pointed out that neglecting the self will eventually lead to a severe identity crisis.

Women find it the most challenging to say no to unpaid caregiving, including mental and emotional load.

'It was a very nuanced NO but never a direct NO,' says Nidhi, when I ask her about how she says no to unpaid caregiving. 'My work is very important to me—it is my identity so I eventually learnt to delegate housework. I learnt that there was nothing wrong in expecting more from my spouse, but it took time for me to able to utter no and ask for him to step up.'

We don't ask for help enough. So, we must ask and not assume that by asking for help, we are somehow letting ourselves down, or that saying no makes us less likeable. Men have survived for generations without giving two hoots about these society-imposed limitations (they have their own, of course, but when we compare the list, it is no wonder they are able to cope with the patriarchal pressures while women are struggling or drowning.

A research paper, 'Unfolding Unpaid Domestic Work in India: Women's Constraints, Choices, and Career' on caregivers says that while unpaid work 'is an important aspect of economic activity and is indispensable for the well-being of individuals, households, and in fact, for the economy as a whole', women are often marginalized in the workplace because of 'their socio-economic position in society to carry out unpaid household activities in the family in the form of cooking, cleaning, fetching food, water, and firewood and giving care'.[6]

This norm makes it more challenging for women to assert their own needs and preferences, including the ability to say no. Susan Faludi, in her work 'Backlash: The Undeclared War Against American Women', highlighted how women who asserted themselves often faced backlash. This is especially true of the workplace—where women have the toughest time saying no or asserting themselves. Women have to pay a 'social cost' for being assertive and are often penalized for asking for better salaries or promotions.[7] [8]

For Mridvika, it was important to say no as a woman entrepreneur. 'For example, investors want to invest in you only if you do the work their way. But I am very clear about what I am building and have said no to some of those asks,' she says.

One investor wanted her to transform her organization into a non-profit business and run a training business for women in Tier Two and Tier Three cities. 'But I said no because that's not what I was building.'

When it comes to her personal life, she has started saying no more often too. 'Just today, I told my partner that I need to rest and can't take the kids to their activity and that he should do it. I spend most of my days running around with my kids to and from various activities—weekends, I have learnt to claim as mine.'

Katharine O'Brien, a postdoctoral research associate at the Baylor School of Medicine, and Eden King of George Mason University, conducted a series of studies in 2014, which found that women had a hard time saying no to extra work in a professional setting, owing mostly to social norms that guided their behaviour. When women turn down requests or say no, not only does it make them feel more guilty but they face backlash from their managers.

'Anecdotal evidence from popular culture suggests that women have a difficult time declining professional requests made by others,' the study said, adding that the 'results confirmed that women do not feel that they can say "no" in the workplace and that this relates to other personality differences and outcomes.'[9]

In intimate relationships, the women's ability to say 'no' is intricately connected to issues of consent, which is crucial to any sexual relationship and yet, women's consent is often assumed in such situations. Gender roles have already decided that as a sexual partner, a woman must be subservient to the man and this makes saying 'no' that much more difficult in intimate relationships leading to abuse.

Priya's transformation also involved saying no to forced sex. She didn't think she could say no, and then she did. 'I started sleeping in a different room and I walked out of that marriage a year later. For a whole year, I wouldn't let him touch me,' she says.

An important part of saying no is the ability to say no to toxic relationships and ending bad marriages.

'I struggled with my insecurities of being lost without a man in my life. I jumped into a relationship and marriage with a rock-solid banker to fill the loss of losing my dad. I should have gone to the US as a free person, travelled, met different people, not committed so soon, processed the grief of my dad, etc. Instead, from the day he died till I was fifty, I always sought relationships to feel "whole" and believed that a man in my life was necessary,' says Dipsikha. 'It is only in the past three years that I have genuinely started loving all of me—not just the physical aspect but the weaker mental parts of my mind as well.'

Subuhi Safvi, a trauma recovery coach, noticed a pattern within herself—that of staying in bad or abusive relationships. After she left her abusive partner in 2014, she ended up in a similar relationship around seven months later. 'It wasn't a healthy relationship and when it ended, I finally took stock. Realizing that all my adult romantic relationships had been unhealthy with some being very clearly abusive was a shock. But it was what propelled me toward healing,' she says. 'I started with self-compassion, which was difficult.

I have, as far as I can remember, had a terribly critical voice in my head telling me everything I do is wrong, that I am worthless and everyone dislikes me or makes fun of me. I went on to gently heal parts of me and today, I can say without a doubt that I am actually happy, I love myself and my body, I am aware of my capabilities, and I am really proud of myself. I am in a healthy relationship, I am doing well professionally, and most importantly, I am a good parent to my dogs.'

Walking out of bad marriages or toxic relationships is the hardest 'no' a woman is required to say. My friend, Divya, walked out of her marriage after nineteen years. I had seen her struggling with this relationship for many years. She would talk about leaving her husband often and then, would just backtrack—sometimes for her children, sometimes for her family. The basis of her decisions would always be the invisible 'what will people say syndrome'—the one syndrome that single-handedly stops most Indian women from living their best lives. Today, Divya is a single mother, her ex-partner does not help her financially (something she agreed to because she wanted a quick end to her marriage) and yet, she is happier than she has been ever before. Yes, she is still struggling with insecurities and a fear of the future, but she is rid of the hopelessness that comes with being in a toxic relationship and a bad marriage.

How to walk out of bad marriages?

'By the courage of conviction and self-worth. Women have to believe they deserve better to walk out of a bad marriage,' says Dipsikha.

Yes, but that belief has to be built over time since any belief we may have in ourselves has been systematically broken down by our society. This is why women stay in bad relationships—believing it to be their fault and that they are not worth anything better.

'When I was younger, I wanted to be in a relationship so badly. I wanted to be loved because I did not think I was lovable at all. When I was with my abusers, I was just so happy they loved me at all that I'd have forgiven any abuse, and I did many times. The first time he hit me, I cried in his arms because even though I knew it was wrong, I still thought I deserved it somehow,' says Safvi. 'I finally got out because I realized if I stayed, I would die. Till the veil lifted from my eyes, I thought it was just me and I deserved all of it. I tried a thousand times before I could walk out. That's how hard it is.'

But, also, love and respect yourself as much as you have been taught to love and respect others; build your confidence just the way you have been taught to be a rock for your family, say no without guilt just the way you have been taught to accept no without questioning, question and probe your guilt—is it really yours? Personally, remember that by saying no to all these extra demands on your time, you are saying yes to the things which are perhaps invisible but no less important—like your mental health, your physical well-being, rest and leisure—some very basic human rights.

A few months ago, a friend confided in me about her relationship—she was not sure but suspected that it was emotionally abusive. I suggested she make a list of how her partner makes her feel each day of the month. 'If in a month, he makes you feel shit about yourself most days and good days are few and far between, then is he worth investing your energy in?' I told her. Making a list of the things you say yes to because you couldn't say no works much in the same way. When at the end of the month, I go through my yes/no list, I always feel more empowered because I know exactly what I will not do the next month. It's a long process because unlearning is cumbersome—there's some corner of ourselves which will pipe up over and over again trying to drag us back to the rabbit hole of what we have grown up believing, how we have fashioned our lives based on those beliefs, and how our aims and goals surrounding what our life should look like is actually not written by us, but by someone else who doesn't even share our gender. I can tell you one thing with certainty though—keep making those lists, and some months down, you will know exactly what you need to change in your lives.

If you are losing yourself in the process of keeping everyone else happy, is it even worth it? You are not coffee, pizza or even chai—you don't need to keep everyone happy. It's not your job. Instead, focus on yourself—do you feel at peace with yourself? How many times a day do you pull yourself down before anyone else can do it? And even after wringing yourself out—are you able to make everyone happy? Many times, in fact, in trying to please everyone, we lose ourselves. And this is a bottomless dark hole—more like quicksand—there's no end to it and there's no way to not sink. The pursuit of pleasing everyone is like trying to negotiate the Lucknowi Bhool Bhulaiya (maze)—stressful. How many times have you tried to do the right thing and yet, people have been upset or not appreciative enough? Too many times, right? This is why saying no becomes so important—because when your family or your acquaintances (including co-workers) know that you are able to set boundaries and say no, your 'yes' will become that much more valuable. Saying no is important to make contributions count and to put a value to yes.

Many women are only able to start saying no after they hit their forties—maybe because as women mature, they develop a greater sense of purpose and conviction that make them more assertive.

'I could never say no to either attending or hosting gatherings. You know how important they are for Indian families, right?' Mridvika says. When it was her birthday two weeks ago, everyone was expecting her to host a dinner for family and friends. But she didn't want to slave it out in the kitchen on her birthday and instead, wanted to spend the day with her children. Then she said what she couldn't on many occasions before—she said 'no'. 'Maybe I was judged for it but I have come to a stage in my life where that doesn't matter any more because I am learning to value myself more. I wanted a relaxed birthday that was about prioritizing myself, but it didn't lessen my love for my family and friends—it just meant that I have learnt to love myself a little bit more and have started to listen to myself more. And I wanted a quiet dinner.'

As I listened to her, I had the sense that I almost always do when I listen to a woman's lived experiences. There are so many moments of 'yes, me too' in these conversations.

There was a time when I, too, couldn't say yes to myself. For years, I would work throughout the day and then slave in the kitchen for some get-together. And while I enjoyed having friends around, the anxiety and the labour that went with it was beginning to grate on me. Even when our friends pitched in with food and other arrangements, the mental load was all mine. Then one day, my son, Che, asked me: 'What do you really want to do for your birthday?' This was a loaded question. Because my birthday falls on New Year's Eve, I have always felt this pressure to have friends over—not so much for my birthday but to ring in the new year together. And yet, that had meant that I would be slaving in the kitchen and manically cleaning the house in preparation for the guests. So when Che asked me this simple question, it set off a thought spiral in my mind. But the answer was really simple. 'I want to stay in bed with a book and the television remote on hand, with a glass of wine and takeout in the evening. I don't need a surprise birthday cake at midnight or a fancy meal in a restaurant and definitely not a get-together.' And that was it. I have been doing this for my last few birthdays and it has been blissful. Saying yes to yourself really is—as my teenage son would say—sick!

But there was something else, too, that brought about this transformation. When I wrote my first book, it was a therapeutic journey for me. Through the women I met and featured in my book, putting down my own most intimate thoughts and feelings in black and white was a cleansing experience. It was like I was looking at my life through the lens of the other and I understood exactly why so many women are now taking up journaling. The other thing that played an important role in my ability to say no was that over the last few years, I also watched many of my women friends trying to have it all and do it all, and not being able to say no. When I began to watch them more closely, I felt keenly how identical our lives were. I took a step back—I took many steps back—and those steps brought me to the word 'no'. And to 'yes'. Yes to myself—to loving myself, listening to myself, making time for myself and caring for myself.

And here's what I have learnt from my journey:

Begin by reflecting on what really matters and what you could let go.

Reflect on what matters to you, and not to others.

Practice saying no—like everything else, saying no is a skill that you build up over time.

Communicate clearly what you need without feeling guilty or defensive.

Politeness is fine but a blunt 'no' is better.

Prioritize yourself.

Paromita Bardoloi, a trauma coach based in Assam, says it's a cycle. 'Once your trauma has healed, you start working on self-love. When you have built up your self-esteem, you will not give in to toxicity. Self-love is about taking small healthy steps—meditation, waking up early, going for a run or any light exercise, opting for therapy, etc. When you start listening to your inner voice and honouring that voice, you will be able to set boundaries and start saying no. If you don't honour and take care of yourself, you will be stuck in another toxic cycle.'

'Saying *no* is just practice,' says a life coach. 'There's no special technique involved. It's simply about understanding that you're not at fault. Perhaps in the past, you handled all the household duties, and now you're exhausted and no longer wish to continue in the same way. The important step is to clearly express this change in your feelings and needs.'

'Don't feel guilty,' she says. 'If you need help with the children, you have to ask your partner. It isn't a favour because the children are the responsibility of both parents.'

The power of no is as important as the art of saying yes—saying yes to the right things in life, that is. I have noticed that by saying no to the right things, I have created the space for saying yes more and more to the right things by default. By turning down an assignment that paid peanuts but expected the world of me in terms of the work, I have, instead, been able to say yes to attending some piano lessons, martial arts class, or even brainstorming some book ideas. 'I am saying yes more. I used to be very tentative if there was any opportunity and self-doubt would set in immediately,' says Nidhi. 'I was always second-guessing myself. But when I started saying yes to the right things, there was no stopping me. It might sound dramatic but that's exactly how it was. I was being adventurous, doing things I had never done before, taking risks, saying no and prioritizing myself. I kept surprising myself.'

When I started prioritizing myself, my first reaction was that of surprise—the world was still rotating on its axis and all was well around me! It was such an unusual experience for me that in the beginning, I would take baby steps—much like rolling out a pilot episode of a series. But then, when the pilot was a hit, the rest of the series kept getting renewed for new seasons on autopilot. 'Like so many women who reach a certain age, I started to care a whole lot less about what others thought of me and a whole lot more about what *I* thought of myself,' Suzanne Gerber wrote in her article 'Why Even Strong Women Sometimes Have a Hard Time Saying No' in 2012. 'Being a people-pleaser and a hedger wasn't making me happy. And funny thing: I found that the more I said no, the easier it got to both say it and stick to my guns when challenges arose.'[10]

So why do we have such a hard time saying no? Because of social conditioning, yes, but also because we are people-pleasers. Not a clinical term exactly, people-pleasing describes a behaviour where a person consistently seeks to please others, often at the expense of their own needs. It goes beyond occasional adaptations in social interactions and involves a strong urge to be what others want them to be. Signs of people-pleasing include difficulty saying no, taking on excessive commitments, avoiding conflict and neglecting one's own needs. Causes can include low self-esteem, anxiety, conflict avoidance, cultural influence, inequity, personality disorders and trauma. People-pleasers may experience stress, frustration and a lack of self-care as they prioritize others over themselves.[11]

'I have reached the stage where I am able to say no, but that doesn't mean that I am unbothered by "letting people down"—that is something I am still working on. I am trying to love and respect myself as much I love and respect others,' one of my interviewees told me.

In 2022, a survey of 1,000 U.S. adult citizens found that a large majority of women self-identified as people-pleasers. And the people-pleasing behaviour they exhibit? Putting other people's needs first at the expense of their own, feeling like they can't say no when someone asks for something and being overly sensitive about how others feel.[12] We still do not have enough studies on Indian women—I hope that this changes in the future, so that we can understand how this socialization works out, sometimes in dangerous ways, in patriarchal societies. Sometimes, women don't say no because of fear of reprisal and violence, and these instances are not just part of abusive relationships but also of a country like ours where casual violence against women is normalized, especially in families. Being liked is a preoccupation with most of us, and with it, comes people-pleasing. In a world dominated by men, women who say 'no' are not likeable.

'It's not so much that it's more important for women to say no, but rather, it can be more challenging for women to do so. From a young age, children are generally encouraged to be agreeable and say yes, and women often face even greater pressure in this regard. This pressure is rooted in the traditional image of women being docile and well-behaved, a stereotype that has been ingrained in society for years. As a result, women often struggle to assert themselves and say no,' says Dr Yadav. 'Women tend to be people-pleasers due to this societal conditioning. However, it's crucial for them to learn to say no because in doing so, they are essentially saying yes to themselves and to the things that truly matter to them. Establishing healthy boundaries is a process that requires practice and skill development. This typically happens through therapy sessions—the first step is gaining awareness of what you want to say yes to and what you need to say no to. This self-awareness is key. Then, you work on developing assertiveness. Often, there are limiting beliefs that hold individuals back from asserting themselves, and these need to be addressed as well. It's a comprehensive process that requires deep exploration and work.'

Hence, the process of learning and unlearning is complicated and time-consuming. With time, more and more women are identifying this and starting their own journeys of unlearning—we will get there soon.

'It's difficult. Women find it so easy to say yes to everything because we have to keep people happy. Saying no means establishing boundaries, doing what makes you happy and focusing on yourself,' says a friend.

Have you ever noticed how easily men say no? There is a power in doing that. Many would say it's due to the basic difference between women and men—women are nurturers, emotional and kind, while men are brass and in your face. It is, however, society which has taught us these differences in how men and women should be. When a situation requires a no, why should we say yes? And yes, it is a process of learning and unlearning, but we must start probing it. Being able to say no is a power move that all women need.

I remember this park called Alton Towers in London, where I had gone with a few friends while I was studying there. The year we visited the park, I remember it had some roller coaster that simulated the feeling of flying. For those who are born with chains on their feet, flying is an anomaly. The feeling of flying was quite new to me as well—I was puce in the face and couldn't wait for it to be over. I also remember looking at the pictures that were taken by the park's cameras during these rides—in them, my facial expressions were enough to show what flying means to people who have always been constrained; the pure joy of letting go was in every grain of those pictures—and I cherish them still. Shallow as it might sound, when I was up there suspended in gravity, I learnt how to let go, how to be and how to accept the hand that was dealt to me.

As someone once told me: 'If people can't love the person you are when you say no, they don't deserve the person you are when you say yes.'

3

Redefining Having It All

'We expect women to work like they don't have children and raise children as if they don't work.'

—Amy Westervelt

There was a time when I deeply cared about having it all—in fact, it was the only goal I was running towards (with blinkers on). I wanted to be the best at everything, more specifically, to effortlessly balance my career and caregiving. It felt ridiculous that I should not strive to balance it all; inconceivable to leave a messy home when I left for work or to not immediately start clearing up when I got back home; implausible for me to not cook up a storm when we were having people over—and not just any storm, the absolute best storm; and unimaginable that I would feed my son or his friends anything but home-cooked food made from the freshest of ingredients without a touch of any ready spices or sauces. I have never been very competitive, but post-marriage, finding myself at the heart of a family that I had to 'nurture', I realized very soon, that to have it all, I must do it all. And yes, it was thrilling and challenging in the beginning in a 'look-I-am-doing-it-all-like-my-mother-without-breaking-a-sweat' manner, but soon it was what it was—a crown of thorns. After two decades of constant burnout, anxiety, spiralling depression, deep exhaustion and never feeling enough, I paused. I knew it was time to redefine what having it all really meant to me as a person in the context of my life and dreams.

No one expects men to have it all because there are no 'ors' in their lives—just 'ands'. Professional and personal, work and family, children and job. But for women, it is always 'either/or'. My personal journey from wanting to have it all to not caring about having it all was a long one, which started when I was in my forties and the mere thought of all that hustle for the rest of my life started to feel debilitating. Mentally I feel so old and exhausted—older than my forty-six years. I am so ready to give up, give in, and hang up my boots and yet, in my mind, I know it's too early to do that. I am forty-six and not seventy-six, and yet, the thought of life on the grind gives me the chills. The official retirement age in our country is sixty—when the government deems you ready to hang up your boots after spending four decades working. With that calculation in mind, and the fact that I have worked at double the pace at work and at home, I should have ideally hung up my boots when I was around thirty. But I did manage to wring out another sixteen years. For all practical purposes, I am done by now. There have been many stop-and-think moments in my life regarding this madness of 'having it all', and all of them contributed to the me that I am now, who can easily ignore the mess at home till someone else clears it up, or who doesn't think too much about ordering take-out or using ready spices to cook. One of those moments came years ago when my son was still a toddler and one of his friends had come home. The little boy loved pasta—his mother had told me. So, I made very good pasta (yes, yes, I pulled out all stops—handmade pasta, slowly simmered sauce . . . I am rolling my eyes at the mere memory). The kid was a foodie, and I don't know why but it was supremely important for me that he liked the pasta I cooked. So, I stood next to him with bated breath. He spooned some pasta in his mouth and even though he didn't spit it out exactly, he might have done so metaphorically. 'I don't like this pasta. Don't you have the one that you can get from the store and just add water and it is ready?' he asked. I didn't know what he was talking about! We slowly realized that he was talking about the instant pasta that was then available in all the stores. I was mortified. His mother—a superwoman and a supermom like me—was mortified as well. And it was then that I realized that kids don't care about how much effort you are putting into their food, but they sure do care about how much time their parents are spending with them. When I weighed the two against each other, my attempt at being a supermom felt vacuous and empty.

'I find it frustrating when people ask successful women if they can "have it all" because this question is rarely posed to men. The notion of having a balanced life is evolving, especially among younger people, who may not prioritize traditional family structures. Not everyone wants to get married or have children; some may find fulfilment in their careers or with a partner and friends,' says Aanchal, a young woman in her mid-twenties.

The term 'having it all' applies only to women—in terms of what they are able to achieve in their personal and professional lives. What is surprising is that this idea of women having it all—basically balancing work and family with beautiful smiles pasted on their faces—gained traction in the 1900s but is still going strong even after so many waves of feminism. We are still expecting women to aspire to have it all instead of trying to redefine it through the lens of our own lived experiences, which has been an absolute disaster.

The concept of having it all plays into the perfection trap that women have to struggle with throughout their lives—into the various guilts that women have to live with throughout their lives, such as the mother's guilt or the daughter's guilt. This concept of having it all is the foundation of all that ails modern women today and plays into the Barbie Doll syndrome. The Barbie doll, introduced by Mattel in 1959, set unrealistic standards for societal perceptions of femininity, beauty and achievement. And what about Barbie's extensive range of careers and lifestyles? Was it aimed at inspiring young girls to have a career or indoctrinating them into the having-it-all-all ideal? Did we not all grow up aspiring to have lustrous hair, long legs and flat stomachs like Barbie, retaining our femininity for the male gaze while also jet-setting around the world, dazzling everyone with our professional success? Women must all be like Barbie dolls—they should be good to look at, have babies but not look like mummies (at best, they can be 'yummy mummies'), be the perfect daughters, wives and mothers, and work around the clock without the hint of a complaint. In fact, it is completely essential that women enjoy this slogging, so let's give them an award—superwoman. And we all gladly slog it out, proud of being superwomen, supermom.

Having it all is the biggest con that has been imposed on women starting to work. The biggest no we will ever say is the one we say to having it all or being a superwoman.

We need to cancel having it all just for it being so non-inclusive.

During my conversations with women from across the country, it was clear that women were ready to change the definition of having it all.

'Till a few years back I thought having it all was just working all the time,' one told me. 'Today, I think having it all means taking a step back, enjoying a leisurely walk in the park, having the time to watch a movie or read a good book.'

Women have been told never to prioritize themselves and that is why, till now, having it all has always come with the subtext of 'giving it all' or 'doing it all'. But hey! Women are seeing through this con now and are taking back control of what should be their 'having it all' life.

'What does having it all really mean?' a friend asked me once. 'Having it all would mean that I get treated at home the same way as men or like any other competent worker at work beyond my gender. It means my success or failure at work is not being perceived as the outcome of my sexuality or the lack of it, nor the consequence of my gender. Most importantly, I can only have it all when I can travel/commute/work/live safely without the fear of being assaulted by predators.'

Bardoloi says that women have been socialized to believe that their worth lies in giving birth, providing free labour in the house or land and sexual favours for their husband—'it is a feudal system where the women belong to the men. And this is where this fantasy was created that women only need a family and the love of their husbands. There was no concept of women having an equal marriage. This picture has been sold to women for generations through songs and stories, media, through movies—when that is the narrative that has been thrown at you forever, how do women break out of it overnight?'

She is right, and that is why we are still struggling. The first step towards rejecting this ridiculous notion of having it all is to start talking about it and sharing our experiences with other women, to understand that you are not alone in this, and that this con has been imposed on women all over the world. Which con, you ask? The one aimed at keeping women constrained to their reproductive roles in society despite the fact that they are also contributing substantially to productive labour or the one created to guard against the decimation of the power structure where men are important because they are the providers. Because if a woman can provide as well as care, then what do they need men for?

What women need to do is start talking about what they want. Not all women want children or a husband. Some might want to travel, while some might want to be single. It's not every woman's dream to be changing diapers or waking up at 3 a.m. to make lunch boxes.

'Does that make me a bad woman or a bad person?' asks Bardoloi. No, but that's what having it all is supposed to do—create this belief in women's minds that if they do not cater to their caregiving responsibilities, they are 'bad women'.

'All changes come with basic conversations. What you are doing right now with this book is igniting a fire that will become a wildfire in the years to come. These are the kind of books people will read,' Bardoloi says. 'The first and most important step to begin this conversation is to tell what we want. Let's use social media to initiate these conversations since every other medium is owned or controlled by men. Let's keep the conversations going, and the fire of our conversations, of sharing of our lived experiences, will destroy the expectations of what women are supposed to be and show them the promise of what we could be.'

The traditional meaning of having it all—husband, children, job, being a career diva along with a domestic goddess—is an archaic concept, especially in a world defined by diverse gender and sexual identities, chosen families, and a gradual disenchantment with the institution of marriage. Redefining it is of paramount importance for women to live a more fulfilled life.

'For me, family is chosen mostly,' says Nitasha Biswas, who won India's first Trans Beauty Contest in 2017. 'We are defined by predetermined and heteronormative ideas of what a family should look like. But my own experience taught me that family is not just people connected by blood—it is where you find yourself most protected and at peace; where you are accepted and loved for who you are and with all your shortcomings. Where you feel like you belong.'

'The concept of having it all is stuck in a time warp,' says Shalaka, an entrepreneur and one of the many women I interviewed for this book. 'Having it all definitely needs to be redefined. For example, I don't need or want children. And yet, I believe I have it all. It is time to rewrite the definition of having it all based on individual experiences. I live in the moment; I should have enough money to travel and do my choice of work, that's all for me. And the most important is that I really want to give back to the society in whatever way possible.'

Shalaka left her high-flying corporate career to work as a solo entrepreneur, helping build brands for tech firms, venture capitalists (VCs), leaders, NGOs, start-ups, etc., because that's what makes her happy and for her, right now, having it all means being able to prioritize her happiness.

'For me, the meaning of having it all has evolved over time, too,' says Pratima, an entrepreneur in her mid-twenties. For her, having it all means having the time to rest and take care of herself so as to 'nurture wholesome relationships while also working, because financial independence is important.' Financial independence also allows women to say no to what's not working and explore other options. 'Someone could be working in the technology sector, but they might also have a passion for baking. If she has enough money, she could explore her passion. She could use her savings to do what makes her happy. Having it all should not just mean being the CEO or founder of a company or a high-flying job,' she says. 'The picture of having it all for women needs to change.'

Having it all should, most importantly, mean a peaceful, mostly free life.

For Priya, having it all now means having a calm mind, since that's what she had to sacrifice when she was trying so hard to keep the mirage of having it all intact. 'When I was married even though the relationship was so abusive, I still craved to have it all. I wanted a perfect relationship, so I kept trying to make it work. And it bothered me that it was not working—my peace of mind was shattered like I was failing some test.'

'We need to really decode what having it all means or rather should mean,' says Saloni, a life coach. 'You might want to have a high-flying corporate career while somebody else might want to work in the social sector to change lives or someone might just want to be. This whole process is about unlearning and undoing social conditioning. I have clients in their thirties who have so much pressure to get married, and whose ideas of having it all extend beyond marriage and children. So, ask yourself what having it all means to you. Forget about what it means for the world, your friends or acquaintances. For me, for example, it really means enjoying every moment. Being fully present. Being completely at peace with who I am.'

We have to undo the socialization of women that leads to this having-it-all-all syndrome. 'Both women and men have to take responsibility for what they want their lives to look like. Men also have a nurturing energy or the so-called feminine energy, but they are not encouraged to explore their nurturing side,' Saloni adds. 'Fathers need to lead by example. If a child grows up seeing fathers helping their mothers, that becomes the norm.'

'Having it all is like the biggest bullshit ever told. I don't know what it means,' Nidhi says. 'Is it something that you can actually compute or calculate?'

What does having it all really mean? Is it about having a perfect work and home life? Is it about being always put together? Is it about not having a hair out of place, not a single crease in your clothes or a frown on your brows? Is it about accepting all the crap that's regularly thrown our way with a smile? Or is it really just about that framed picture on the desk—of a smiling, happy, perfect family? If you ask me, it's none of the above. For me, having it all sometimes is just being able to put my feet up and read a book or watch a show. Even though women have always known in their hearts what having it all means to them, it is only now that we are challenging the definition that has been dumped on us for so long.

This is a silent movement, an invisible protest; mostly personal at the moment, but it will soon become a revolution worth reckoning. Redefining having it all, for me, is the most important intervention that a woman can take in her life.

For Mridvika, having it all has evolved with time. 'Earlier, having a career, settling and having a family was important—it meant the world to me. But as I have progressed in life, I do not necessarily want to have it all at the same time.' she says. She no longer wants the pressure to be a 'super time manager'—always hustling, making every minute count and trying to fit into spaces. She is okay with being an average mother and spouse on the days she prioritizes her work and vice versa. 'I have normalized that for myself.'

But change is possible, and like Bardoloi rightly points out, it will come out of conversations and actions that women take themselves. As someone told me, the first step of dismantling the toxic idea of having it all will have to come from our mothers. 'If we grew up seeing our mothers prioritizing themselves, that is what we would have learnt too. We could also permit ourselves to redefine what is expected of us. For example, I would want to normalize takeaway food for family gatherings, but if my mother holds on to the belief that cooking tons of food at home is the only way to show love and respect to guests, I will never have the courage to take that decision on my own and I, too, will recreate that in my own life. It takes one person in the family to challenge norms, man or woman.'

Women today are feeling the pressure of having it all—thanks to social media and the online boom, women also have access to more resources and information, and are in a process of unlearning, even if they do not often realize this. There is a conscious and unconscious unlearning that is going on among women all over the world—and it is happening not a moment too soon.

Women, globally, are under a lot of pressure. They're expected to be good at their jobs, cook healthy food, keep their house clean, and take care of their kids. Their spouses or partners, who are only focused on their jobs, rarely realize how hard this is. Even though times have changed, some old ideas about who should do what in a family haven't changed as much. And it is up to the women to change that because they are the worst affected by it. Here's an idea—instead of striving to have it all, *let's change it all*.

'Women have to stop taking pride in their multitasking abilities as a superpower. Any intelligent person is able to multitask, but men have found a way to weaponize their incompetencies,' says Bardoloi.

'Men will go to the kitchen and say "I can't do this." They will burn the rotis and the women will quickly take over. Don't do that—ask him to order a takeout instead. If it's his turn to provide food for the family, he has to do it in whichever way that works for him,' Bardoloi says. 'Teach your sons to cook and teach your daughters about financial literacy.'

When Nidhi started saying no to doing it all just to retain the façade of her 'having it all', it was a nuanced 'no' to begin with as explained earlier.

'Even when things were falling apart around me, I said no to doing it all,' she says. 'I learnt how to manage my emotions without feeling like I had to be the one to do everything.'

When Nidhi started her entrepreneurial journey, she wasn't making money right off the bat. 'It took some time for people to understand the importance of my work,' she says. 'I remember my husband's face when he came to one of my events and there were like 300 people there. I could see that it was at that moment the realization struck him that I was doing something for myself which was also important and I needed support.'

For Nidhi, multitasking is not a virtue. She doesn't take pride any more in juggling a multitude of things and ending her day harried and exhausted. And most importantly, she is *talking* about it—about how she feels about all the expectations of her. She moves meetings around and no longer has a chock-a-block calendar with appointments, which means she is also not completely drained at the end of each day. 'I am now very clear about what I want for myself and what works for me,' she adds.

Mridvika is building an organization that aims to address gender inequalities, especially in the workspace. The irony of the fact that, in her household, the mental burden is on her, is not lost on her. 'It's still a struggle,' she says. 'I am right now in Ahmedabad volunteering with a non-profit for a week with my ten-year-olds. They had an orientation at their school, which I had asked my husband to attend. The event was to start at 8.30 a.m. and when I called him in the morning, he said he had forgotten about it.'

But Mridvika doesn't have the luxury of forgetting these things—because she doesn't want to be labelled a bad mother or want her children to face the consequences of her not having things under her control. 'I make sure that their books, stationery, uniforms, bags, everything is labelled, covered and so on. Of course, there are certain things I can do better than him, and I do not want to make any points at their expense, but I realize that I do need to pull back somewhat for my partner to step up,' she says.

Mridvika was recently travelling out of town for a work trip for two weeks. 'I didn't check in as much as I would generally and they figured it out themselves. So, there are certain things I have to remind myself to let go of. And there are some things where I'm guilty of saying, "Let me only do it. I know I can do it better."'

Many women in their early or late forties or younger are bringing up their children teaching them that household chores are gender neutral. My son, Che, is as apt at doing chores outside of the home as he is at home. And what I find heartening is that he is keen to learn. A friend's son is super proud of his skills in the kitchen—his particular expertise is making grilled cheese sandwiches. And whenever he has been over to stay, he has made it a point to make one for me and the rest of the family. Just seeing him effortlessly negotiating the kitchen makes me hopeful that we are breaking through the gendered barriers of productive and reproductive work. 'My kids have been brought up knowing chores are gender agnostic,' says Natasha. 'Though my husband is old school, he knows he should ask and not demand. I also don't attempt to do it all any more. I deal with mental load by being aware of it and delegating it when it gets too much.'

I have also started letting go of many things. Recently, I started working full-time again and I am at work the whole day. I have always tended to pick up full-time work in between freelance stints, especially when I would feel there was a need or that I had enough help for me to step away for a major part of the day. During my earlier full-time stints, I would call home many times to check if things were okay, reminding my husband and son of things they needed to do. But I don't do that any more. And guess what? The household runs just fine. My partner and son figured out the stuff—in the beginning, they would make a mess, eat the wrong food or get the wrong food cooked, but I learnt to ignore that and eventually, they knew how to do it. In fact, I learned from them that it was perfectly fine to make the wrong decisions—the earth won't swallow you; that if you ate breakfast for lunch and lunch for dinner, it was still fine; and that sometimes, instant noodles were a great palate cleanser from all the organic and home-cooked food that I feel compelled to cook or get cooked every day. I only needed to leave them alone for them to figure it out because, as I keep reiterating, running a house is just a life skill. *Anyone can do it.*

The need to change the definition of having it all really resonates with the modern woman, who is overworked at home and burnt out at work, and they are unwilling to pass it down to the next generation. 'I hold books like *Lean In*[1] accountable for a lot of mental health issues for women. We cannot have it all, and when you dig deep, you realize that the ones who seem to have it all too have made choices and don't in fact *have it all* (they also have the privilege of better support systems),' Natasha says. 'Each of us needs to determine how much effort we are willing to put into each of the roles we are expected to play and stick to it. It is not the same for everyone, and as women, we should support the choices of other women.'

Most women I spoke to, about this expectation of women striving to have it all, were scathing in their rejection of it (to my great elation).

'Sometimes, the idea of "having it all" feels more like a daunting expectation than a goal to aspire to. It's almost as if there's an underlying message that women need to juggle everything perfectly or risk losing something vital—and since caregiving is non-negotiable, it has to be their financial independence, right?' says a young woman I interviewed. 'I think, having it all needs to be redefined as doing the best we can, because, believe me, we are just trying to get through the day without falling apart.'

Having it all is also a tone-deaf concept in a world with myriad sexual and gender identities, where chosen families are as important as biological ones and women are not scared to be alone. The old saying that 'you can choose your friends but not your family' doesn't hold true any longer. 'I am single. I have no children. I have never married,' says one of my interviewees. 'Don't tell me I don't have it all, because, for me, I have it all. And that's what's more important. What I believe to be my "all"—not some society(men)-dictated variation of it.'

More and more women are calling out this heteronormative definition of having it all, more young women are resisting the pressure of getting married just for the sake of it and more women are walking out of bad marriages. India currently has the highest number of single women (the rate of divorce has also been on the upswing), and women are making these decisions despite the fact that our society still considers singledom and divorces for women to be blemishes rather than informed choices.

Often, these jibes and judgments come from other women—perhaps, they too are burdened with unhappy relationships but do not yet have the courage to walk out of those relationships. Yet. It is women who are still racing to have it all that pull down women who dare to redefine having it all the hardest.

Ooh! Why do divorced women seem to be having all the fun?

I cringed when an acquaintance, a woman, teased a freshly divorced friend, whose face immediately went pale. I knew the strength she had to gather for years to walk out of that marriage; I knew the conversations she had to have with herself, her family and her children.

I knew of the sleepless nights and her fear of being lonely, and yet, she decided she was worth so much more. And here was someone who was diminished into a shitty jibe—that too, a woman. A modern woman at that.

In an ideal world, the two of them would talk and share their experiences, and maybe, the woman who jeered would have gone away inspired by some of her courage. But unfortunately, that's not how it's been taught by patriarchy—the lingering distrust between women is debilitating and the conditioning that we are nothing without a male 'protector' runs deep. It is this conditioning that makes the strongest of women breadwinners hang onto bad marriages just to feel like they have achieved it all. But the younger generations, women like Shalaka, for example, are changing it all, and not a minute too soon.

'The fact that I am single by choice makes people really uncomfortable. Women especially find it very hard to understand this concept of being single by choice. It's not like there are no men around, but marriage is not a priority for me. I am happy with my life where I am not answerable to anyone. I can make my own decisions. I have the freedom to do whatever I want to and that makes me happy. This confidence gives you the freedom of choice,' she says, adding that marriage should be a choice and not a foregone conclusion. 'A majority of the marriages across age groups that I have seen are unhappy. From my grandparents to my parents, I only see people not getting along. We don't think. We don't question. We need more confident women to question, why is marriage mandatory—"Do I need this?" It's like buying a new phone—do you want it or do you need it? Parents should also allow children to think and decide for themselves. Women should take care of themselves and understand themselves better. Decision-making should not be influenced and currently, it's horribly influenced.'

And yes, most of us grow up seeing our mothers compromise in their marriages. And most often, it is because of the fear of loneliness. But can you be dependent on someone else for your happiness all the time? And is loneliness as bad as it is made out to sound like?

'The narrative about loneliness is manipulative—pushed by social media and dating apps,' says Shalaka. 'And Bollywood—uff! It's just love porn.'

Completely! Look at how the whole marketing and event industry as well as popular media have glamorized weddings—making women crave the 'event' rather than the relationship. Look at the advertisements of glamorous brides—the jewellery, venues, and portfolio of wedding shots with the same dimpled smiles and staring into each other's eyes. Even though young women know it's staged, they crave it for themselves—to be the centre of attention for this one day or week. A dermatologist acquaintance had once told me that women in their mid to late twenties come to her for Botox and fillers before their weddings. 'They all want to look like a Bollywood bride,' she said. And then they make wrong decisions—choose the wrong men, the wrong relationships. But there are many young women like Shalaka who are seeing through this now and are not scared to be alone. They are not waiting for 'the one'. Recently, Shalaka met a young man who wanted to date her. She was kind but didn't beat around the bush and told him that she was not open to dating currently. 'He was appalled when he heard that,' she says. 'But there is a need to normalize the fact that I won't date just to fit in. I will date only when the time is right and I am in the right headspace.'

If you ask me, this emphasis on marriage has only worsened women's condition in this country.

'When I was twenty-seven, everyone was asking me why I wasn't getting married. At home, my family was worried. At work, my boss was worried. Then they would say, "It's because of your dark skin and so, you should be more submissive and just say yes to whoever says yes to you,"' Priya says. 'And look where all that marriage advice got me.'

But Priya is also blamed for the failure of her marriage.

'My mother-in-law used to tell me not to talk to my parents about the abuse. She told me it was my fault. And I believed her and did not tell my parents ever. I didn't know how to cook so she would say, "You don't cook well or dress well so he doesn't like you. You are too thin. Men like curves." She would tell me all sorts of things to convince me that it was all my fault,' Priya says. 'So she placed the onus of the success of the marriage on me. For a long time, I was convinced and stayed in the marriage trying to make it work, trying to change myself so that it would work.'

Priya feels young women should have the confidence that they can make it work alone too. 'Don't get married because of the pressure or because you think no one else is going to come along,' Priya said.

'Women can make it work alone too. Even if they have children. What kept me from walking out of my marriage was the fear that perhaps, I was not capable enough to survive on my own or look after the kids. But I learnt that I can, simply by doing it. Don't stay in a bad marriage under the illusion of having it all. Walk away, especially if you have children. They deserve better.'

And that is the greatest lesson for us all to learn—we deserve better, so much better. And having it all should just mean one thing—being able to live a life free of undue expectations and violence, with adequate and equal access to resources and opportunities. When women have equal control over the resources of a country, that would be a have-it-all moment for them.

When you redefine having it all, you must also redefine how you look at yourself in the mirror—do you like the face that stares out at you? Redefine hating your body, your face or who you are because you don't measure up to some set standards. Whose standards are they? Men's, perpetuated through women. The way a woman must look is decided by the male gaze, but what about your own gaze?

When I look back at my life, I realize that over 98 per cent of it was defined by this myth of having it all. And it was because my mother unconsciously portrayed the wrong image of having it all herself—she had a good job, a perfect relationship, a husband who helped with the children and let her work, and in return, she looked after the family, cooked fresh food, studied with her daughters and attended all family festivities. Yet, what a misleading picture it was. Why did I come to know about my parents' abusive marriage when I was forty-four? Had I known that before, it would have been the end of this rosy picture that went on to define most of my life.

Don't let them tell you that women can't have it all—let me tell you instead that women do not need to have it all.

I am often mortified at the opportunities I wasted in my life when I was running after this myth—when my friends were travelling around Europe, I was jumping from one job opportunity to the other, knowing exactly what I needed to do to have it all at the back of my mind. Then, I had it all, and it came with a lot of stress and exhaustion. And suddenly, I didn't want to have it all. I became a flawed mother and a flawed partner and the ground didn't open and swallow me. My son loved me the same and my partner adored me the same. They didn't even notice the size of the ball I dropped because, you see, over the years, that ball had become a giant ball of expectations. And then I just felt silly! For me, now, having it all means having the time to read two books a month, binge-watching Netflix, going to the gym with my son or just lying around doing nothing with my pooches, Kuttush and Gypsy.

And yes, while work and taking care of my family are still important to me, I am not killing myself over them. I am delegating, prioritizing and trying to do things for myself too—I am trying to redefine having it all. I really think I started the process many years ago when I rejected the expectations of me to work like I have no children and raise my son like I was merely a housewife and became an independent journalist. I worked hard but I worked at my own pace and created opportunities to explore the different facets of having it all—some months it was just prioritizing my child, some months it was work. I played around with this for many years. Drop that ball, please. If dropping that ball makes you unimportant and unnecessary, then you need to know it sooner rather than later.

Aanchal, who identifies as queer, feels that the concept of 'having it all' is changing and that the change is coming from women. 'Women get to define what "having it all" means for them, not anyone else,' she says.

What does it mean to her? 'It means having a fulfilling job, financial stability and minimal conflict or hatred,' she tells me.

'While I haven't personally faced discrimination for being queer, I feel the pressure of being more public about it, especially for the sake of younger generations. There's a responsibility to show younger people that there are individuals in various industries who are open about their identity, so they can feel more comfortable and less insecure about their own journeys.'

Aanchal is right—the notion of 'having it all' for women often carries an additional burden of publicly announcing or discussing their sexual identities. This expectation arises from various factors, including the aspiration to be role models for others facing similar challenges, the drive to challenge stereotypes, and the goal of fostering a more inclusive and accepting society.

Successful women, including those who identify as LGBTQ+, are often seen as torchbearers, expected to lead by example and provide hope and representation to others. By openly acknowledging their sexual orientation, they can help break down harmful stereotypes and demonstrate that one's identity should not limit their potential or success. However, it's essential to acknowledge that coming out or discussing one's sexual identity is a deeply personal choice. No one should feel compelled to do so unless they are comfortable and ready, as the pressure to come out can be a complex aspect of the broader discussion on gender roles, expectations and representation in society.

'Women often feel this responsibility, especially when they are among the first in their industry to be open about their identity. It's like they bear the weight of representing both older and future generations of women. If they make a mistake, it can be perceived as a failure for the entire community. It's a constant struggle,' she says. 'However, the idea of having it all is changing, and women should be able to define it on their terms. The pressure to be open about one's identity exists, especially to support younger generations, but it's a constant challenge and responsibility,' she adds.

Aanchal still doesn't feel that she needs to announce her sexual identity to have it all. 'I am a bisexual woman but I don't announce it to everyone I meet. I don't see why anyone needs to know about my personal life, but the people who matter know.'

And while women do not need to run towards the myth of having it all, they do deserve to have it all—just not in the patriarchal sense of the phrase, which includes a picture-perfect family and a blooming career—all optics that hide overwork and raging inequalities and are non-inclusive to boot. Women need to have it all in terms of access to resources and policies. We need equal pay, affordable childcare, transgender and queer rights, corporate diversity, career support and equal distribution of household chores, including unpaid caregiving. We will embrace having it all when it is not based on the invisible labour of women and is not killing women. We will embrace having it all when we are able to live violence-free lives and our picture-perfect smiles are not hiding deep exhaustion, sleep deprivation or even spousal abuse.

'The "post-feminist" young woman remains unfulfilled. She does everything, is burnt out and tired. So, what is missing? Well, since the dawn of feminism there has been a fight for women's rights and equal opportunities for women in a "man's world",' Linda Elizabeth Chardon argues in her paper, 'The Personal, Political, and the Virtual? Redefining Female Success and Empowerment in a Post-feminist Landscape'. 'Today, we define feminine success in terms of masculine models; we frame our "feminist" triumphs in the language of the patriarchy of society. Popular culture and cultural values have perpetuated these beliefs and reinforced these standards in all aspects of women's lives. Where we should be searching to discover what defines both professional and relational equality for women, we have, as an alternative, borrowed the organizing structures of male hierarchies and applied these systems to females. Women must be as successful as a man would be when it comes to careers. Women must exploit their sexual agency and have many casual sexual partners, as a man would. We view this as power.'

'But what is our post-feminist power?' she asks. 'And if it is "truly our right to choose", we must make choices that fulfil *our* desires and *ourselves* on our own terms.'[2]

We are dissatisfied because we are trying to find our happiness and success within systems built by men, for men. We are searching for equality within patriarchal systems that are built on the oppression and suppression of women. We are trying to fit in when we should rebuild, we are compromising instead of rebelling and we are striving for handouts when half the resources are ours.

Women don't have to choose. They definitely don't have to choose between work or home or children or career. The spectrum of choice is evolving—we need to evolve too.

We are trying to make it in a man's world which runs on men's rules—it's a world made by men, for men. To redefine having it all, we must first dissociate ourselves from these binaries and options that have already been constructed for women and instead, start asking ourselves: *what do I want?*

For women who identify as queer or transwomen, having it all comes with very different expectations. But at the end of the day, as M, a highly accomplished educator and transwoman, says, it comes from her having an education, a job and the courage to live life on her own terms. 'Women are delaying getting married or do not marry at all. The necessity of marriage is not being felt as a result. Because women, with all the jobs and occupations, will still have to exchange vows on their wedding days where they will have to hand over all control to their husbands. It's a ritual they say without thinking too much. That meets the heteronormative normalcy. Maybe that does not exist in our stratum, but that's because the entire strata has been disrupted now,' she says.

'"Having it all" in my life has meant that many people have many hopes and wants pinned on me. Since I have made something of myself, it is expected of me to make something of every transgender person. How is that possible? I have done that with myself through my efforts. People ask, "Why must you work?" My colleagues tell me: "It's your good luck that we have accepted you. You would've been at the traffic signals, otherwise." I feel bad. They do not care what I have achieved. They think they have cleared the path for me,' she says.

'Women learn tricks of deception and camouflage themselves to paint a picture that is expected of them,' she adds. 'But even after 100 years, when two women speak, they're going to share the same struggles.'

4

Escaping the Perfection Trap

'If you look for perfection, you'll never be content.'

—Leo Tolstoy

The first time Priya genuinely felt pretty was when she gave birth to her first child. Throughout her life, Priya had been made to feel like she was not enough just because her complexion was dark. When her parents arranged her marriage with her (now) former partner, she was so overwhelmed that someone was willing to marry her despite the colour of her skin that she did not hesitate to say yes.

'I was always compared to my sisters, who have fairer skin,' says Priya. 'I went through life never feeling enough and feeling embarrassed about the skin I was born into. When my former partner said yes to the marriage proposal, I was so overwhelmed and grateful, that I said yes.'

The irony, however, was that the taunts over her skin colour did not go away after her marriage. Her husband taunted her over it throughout their marriage while her in-laws always felt unhappy because she was not 'pretty' enough for their son. The comments from strangers and acquaintances did not disappear either, but the only thing that changed was that Priya stopped caring about it all.

'I am totally okay with it. I have understood I can't let others decide what should or should not matter to me. I have taken that power back. I used to be thin when I was younger, I am not any more, and I am okay with it.'

Priya was also often advised to stay away from colours that would highlight her dark skin. 'I wear every conceivable colour and colour combination now,' she says with a laugh. 'I love wearing pink or magenta, colours that people would often tell me not to wear as they highlighted my dark complexion.'

The obsession with fair skin is, of course, legendary in India. For generations, we have been crushing over fairness creams. I remember an older girl in my school, fair, pretty and kind of really dreamy-looking, who wanted to be fairer still and carried a tube of a popular fairness cream in her school bag. While I have always thought that was such a vain thing to do, over the years, I have realized that many women, irrespective of class and caste in India, hide fairness creams in their purses and religiously apply them throughout the day. I once wrote a story on this fairness cream obsession in India where I interviewed a woman who suffered extreme side effects from using a fairness cream and yet, she went back to another brand promptly after she recovered.

Nidhi, too, carried a tube of fairness cream in her school bag. Growing up in a small town in Chhattisgarh, she experienced what we can now safely call endless trolling about her skin tone and her weight.

'I was never selected for major roles in school plays, even when I was a good actor who was genuinely interested in the performing arts. They would pick girls who were completely disinterested in the arts but were fair,' she remembers. Her memory takes me back down my own memory lane—a humiliation I think I carry within me to this day. In a school play on *Alice in Wonderland*, I was given the role of a cook, who just stood in a corner and sneezed. The lead part of Alice had gone to a very fair (and hence, beautiful) girl. I did my bit, but it stings me to this day that I was not chosen to play Alice because I was plump and not fair. That was the first time I realized that, as a woman, who I was and what I brought to the table was secondary to how I looked and how well I fit into the accepted narrative of beauty. Nidhi remembers not feeling good in her own skin. 'I remember when I was eight or nine, I would ardently pray to God that when I woke up the next day, I would be fair,' she says.

Just imagine how early this perfection bug bites us; eight or nine is no age for a little girl to be conscious about her complexion or her body type and yet, they are. Maybe because everyone seems to have a say in how women should look and behave, even though they have zero commitment to their social and economic empowerment. This is why so many of us are walking through life feeling like we are not good enough—putting on a brave face and a bright smile, trying to suck in our stomachs, making sure our uneven teeth don't show in a wide smile, hiding behind someone in a group photo, slapping on foundation to hide our acne or concealer to hide our dark circles.

Shaming women is systemic—almost a national pastime.

In 2019, Fortis Healthcare conducted a survey among 1244 women (between the ages of fifteen to sixty-five) across twenty cities (including Delhi NCR, Mumbai, Bengaluru, Hyderabad, Chennai, Amritsar, Ludhiana, Jalandhar, Mohali, etc.).[1] It found that:

- 84 per cent said that they experienced more body shaming as compared to men
- 47.5 per cent reported having experienced body shaming at their school or workplace
- 32.5 per cent reported that their friends often tend to make negative comments about the way they look (be it in terms of their body weight, body shape, skin tone, hair, etc.)
- 76 per cent felt that the media portrayals of beauty contribute towards promoting the prevalence of body shaming

- 90 per cent believed that films and television shows often do tend to make fun of people who do not conform to the standard norms and expectations
- 89 per cent reported feeling uncomfortable about their own selves when they read comments about other people's appearances on social media platforms
- 28 per cent reportedly find it difficult to stand up for themselves when someone criticizes their physical appearance
- 31 per cent reported that they sometimes don't feel like facing the world because of what people would say about their physical appearance
- 66 per cent believed that it is important to look good in order to feel confident
- 62 per cent reported having felt anxious and nervous when people have commented on their looks and physical appearance
- 67 per cent also reported feeling angry because of body shaming

This study was conducted in 2019 and is a grave reflection of how women are constantly made to feel not enough.

Most women go through life battling body dissatisfaction—negative thoughts and feelings about one's body—that leads to various mental health issues. Studies have shown that women experiencing higher levels of body dissatisfaction are at a higher risk of developing mental disorders such as depression, anxiety, eating disorders, body dysmorphic disorder and low self-esteem.[2] Societal pressures, peer influences, body objectification and cultural factors contribute to the association between body dissatisfaction and mental health issues. Understanding this link is crucial for developing interventions that promote body positivity and self-acceptance among women.

Research on body dissatisfaction shows that girls, female adolescents and women of all ages report body dissatisfaction to some degree. Some studies indicate variations in body dissatisfaction across different age groups, while others suggest it remains stable in females throughout adulthood. Body appreciation, on the other hand, tends to be higher in older women. A 2019 paper, 'Body Dissatisfaction, Importance of Appearance, and Body Appreciation in Men and Women Over the Lifespan', found that it was 'a predictor for the development of an eating disorder.'[3]

In my view, as women age, their body dissatisfaction tends to decrease for various interconnected reasons. As we grow older, our priorities shift, and aspects such as family, career, and personal accomplishments take precedence over our physical appearance. This shift in focus naturally diminishes the importance of body dissatisfaction in our lives.

Furthermore, with age comes a greater sense of self-acceptance. We tend to develop a more profound appreciation for our bodies, learning to embrace them as they are and relinquishing the habit of constantly comparing ourselves to societal beauty ideals.

I've also noticed that as we age, the influence of media and societal beauty standards gradually wane.

We become less susceptible to the unrealistic portrayals of beauty in the media, which helps foster a healthier body image.

Additionally, with life experience, our confidence tends to grow. We gain a better understanding of our self-worth beyond mere physical appearance, which contributes to a more positive body image.

Our life's challenges and experiences further equip us with resilience and effective coping strategies. This resilience helps us deal with body image issues more adeptly and reduces dissatisfaction.

Finally, as we accept and even embrace the natural process of ageing, we often develop a more positive perspective on our bodies. Rather than viewing ageing as a negative aspect, we come to see it as a sign of maturity and wisdom, which significantly contributes to a more positive body image overall.

It is important to note that while body dissatisfaction may lessen with age in many women, it is not a universal trend. Individual experiences vary, and some women may still struggle with body image issues as they age. Additionally, more research is needed to fully understand the complexities of body dissatisfaction and its changes over the lifespan in different populations.

Studies have shown that women often bear the burden of unfair societal expectations. A Pew Centre research study found women faced more pressure to be involved parents and more physically attractive than men.[4]

Over the years, I have realized that this is one battle we are never going to win because the expectations of perfection from women are in reality a tool of oppression—it is a way to keep us always on our toes so that we never get too cocky about ourselves. But what if we stop playing by these rules? We will be neutralizing the weapon of our oppression. Would you go and jump in quicksand? No, right? So, well, perfection is that quicksand. Standing in front of the mirror and repeating 'I am perfect' may or may not work, but committing to a process to unlearn socialization and letting go of the obsession to be perfect is a good place to start. When you see it as a trap, you will avoid it. That's where I started. Too many times, I have been told, 'Oh, a little lipstick would brighten up your face so much.' Maybe, but I think my face is fine, and if you were expecting to see a brighter face, I am happy to disappoint.

And because men are the providers and so-called protectors, women have been socialized to cater to their whims over their own wishes. A friend, who abhors wearing high heels, always wears stilettos because her husband likes it. 'It adds height and makes me look slim,' she says. 'It's his impression of how his wife should look, not of me.' Mothers still insist that their daughters, after giving birth, should tie a scarf over their post-partum bellies for months to flatten the stomach. Women are supposed to be mothers, to give birth, and yet they are also expected to erase all signs of what is often painted as an earth-shattering, life-changing event in a woman's life. Reportedly, the women who can afford it are wheeled straight from labour rooms to operation theatres to fix their post-pregnancy bodies. Sadly, women are not allowed to even carry their own stories on their bodies.

Women are subjected to so much shaming over the course of their lives starting from right when they are young that it passes on to the various stages of their lives in different forms—from feeling imperfect about their bodies and their complexion to feeling not enough as daughters or wives or mothers, this vicious cycle has no end. Nidhi was not just shamed for her complexion but also because she was plump. 'I grew up hearing terms like *moti* and *kali*' she says. She was shamed for her dark complexion while she was working at a multinational company. 'We were discussing my upcoming wedding and one of the girls casually said, "You cannot wear pink because it will not suit your complexion."' And while Nidhi had gotten into the habit of ignoring such comments, something shifted in her that day. 'I was like "Hell yeah, I will wear pink."' And she did.

It was when Nidhi moved to Dubai with her partner that she truly embraced herself. 'It was still in my head but I was surrounded by people of different nationalities, skin colours and bodies and my social conditioning wore off organically. You have to understand, there are so many different shapes and forms of people, and they are making it work in the world. You will, too.'

'Is there any woman in this country who has not been body- or complexion-shamed?' asks Mridvika. She grew up alongside a brother, who was lean. 'People would joke in front of me, asking my parents what they fed me that I was so fat. Or they would do one better and ask me questions like "Do you eat all the food so that there is none left for your brother?" They would be so taken with their joke that they wouldn't even notice how my face would pale,' she remembers. 'Time taught me to ignore these comments but they certainly impacted how I began to perceive myself,' she says. Mridvika did many things to fit in—she cut her hair short thinking that tomboys did not have to face such taunts and went on crash diets to be the 'ideal' weight when she was getting married. But sometimes this pursuit of perfection can be deadly, and Mridvika found that when she was carrying her twins and went into preterm labour in her sixth month of pregnancy. 'Thanks to the medical advances we have and the ability to spend on those facilities, both my kids survived and are healthy boys now. But I now realize that my stupid crash dieting had weakened my inner uterine muscles leading to preterm labour. The physical and emotional trauma was indescribable.'

'I now ignore society-approved constructs of how a woman should look,' she says. 'But do I not have certain days when I still feel pressured? I do. When there's a family wedding, I want to look a certain way and wear certain clothes and I pick up a fad diet, join the gym and then fail at all of that. And that's okay. That's what makes us human.'

Yes, that's what makes us human, and understanding that is the first step towards debunking this myth of the perfect woman created by patriarchy. Let perfection be what you want to be not what others want you to be. Because the perfection trap in India, like everything else, is a double, triple, quadruple-edged sword. It requires women to be fair and beautiful, which means you have to be the right size (slim but not too slim—some curves but not too many curves), the right height (not too tall—you don't want to tower above your husband. Short is okay—then you can just be made fun of), long hair, perfect gait and posture (women are still made to walk during marriage viewings), sing like a cuckoo, dance like a maestro, be a domestic goddess but also a glass-ceiling breaker. You have to be the perfect daughter, the perfect wife, the perfect daughter-in-law and the perfect mother. At work, you have to be likeable, not aggressive, willing to take on all extra work with a smile, never complain about sexism or the pay gap and let male workers talk over you at meetings or take credit for your ideas—the expectations of women are uncanny, to say the least.

This myth of perfection has been imposed on women in a very systemic manner. Once work became divided into productive and reproductive labour, men became the workers and women the homemakers or nurturers. And then, there was no looking back after capitalism found a way to exploit women's insecurities, fears and self-perception issues and turned them into business opportunities. Since the movie *Barbie* was released in 2023, I have been thinking about how it has helped dump this unattainable sense of perfection in young girls. I remember buying one almost every year as a kid and being fascinated with her tiny waist, long hair, high heels and long legs. But I was plump, had short hair and no long legs. So, I cut my Barbie's hair short, made her new clothes—loose t-shirts and trousers—and made her my own. But that was just temporary—my tryst with eating disorders also began around the same time. I didn't want to look like Barbie, but I didn't *not* want to either. There are two Barbie dolls sold every second in the world, according to a Get Real Barbie Fact Sheet. The target market for Barbie doll sales is young girls who are 3–12 years of age. A girl usually has her first Barbie by age three and collects a total of seven dolls during her childhood.[5]

The fact sheet says:

> If Barbie were an actual woman, she would be 5'9' tall, have a 39' bust, an 18' waist, 33' hips and a size 3 shoe! Barbie calls this a 'full figure' and likes her weight at 110 lbs. At 5'9' tall and weighing 110 lbs, Barbie would have a BMI of 16.24 and fit the weight criteria for anorexia. She likely would not menstruate. If Barbie was a real woman, she'd have to walk on all fours due to her proportions.

In 1965, Slumber Party Barbie was introduced along with a bathroom scale permanently set at 110 lbs (49 kgs) with a book entitled *How to Lose Weight* with directions inside stating simply 'Don't eat'.[6]

'The absence of self-love often stems from a constant bombardment of societal ideals about beauty and what women should look like. This influence is everywhere, even when not explicitly discussed. Consider how few actresses represent the image of a typical Indian woman. The beauty industry, makeup, and related elements are pervasive, and it's challenging not to be affected by this ongoing conditioning,' says Dr Yadav.

'We have to raise girls to be confident of who they are—both physically and emotionally. We also have to raise our boys to value confidence and personalities and not just surface beauty. Confidence is the new definition of beauty. To bring about this change, we must first address and let go of the beliefs we hold about beauty. I incorporate various exercises into my therapy sessions, such as mirror work inspired by the teachings of Louise Hay. These exercises help in cultivating self-love and gradually lead to the development of self-compassion. There are clear steps to follow in this transformative journey.'

Personally speaking, it has been a struggle for me too, to escape this perfection trap. I have forever struggled with trying to look perfect—to have the perfect weight, the perfect skin, the perfect gait, the perfect hair. I love wearing my hair short and yet, every time someone comments (and they always do) something like 'You have such lovely thick hair, you should wear it long', I start growing it (and eventually cut it short again). I still struggle to love myself in the mirror, but I am better than before and the process continues.

There's not a single day that goes by when I don't consciously work at escaping this trap and teach myself to not care—to be happy in my own skin. Throughout my life, I have been skin colour-shamed (my sister is fair, I am not) and body-shamed ('You would look so beautiful if you just lost a little bit of weight'). I am forever trying to lose weight, trying to look a certain way, and then just like Mridvika did, I, too, realized that it doesn't matter. I don't mind failing the perfection test any more, and seeing all the body positivity around me nowadays really makes me happy. We must make use of this momentum because loving ourselves in the mirror is the first step to a happy and fulfilling life. Many years ago, a friend and very accomplished businesswoman, had posted a picture of her receiving some respected award. Sadly, a majority of the comments on her post were about her weight. I had to jump in and call this out. She was embarrassed and told me it was fine and that she didn't mind. But of course, she did. And I will repeat here what I told her that day—this is a vicious cycle and the only way to escape this trap is to call it out for ourselves and our friends.

The pressure of perfection weighs heavily on women. 'I see women around me who are waking up at three in the morning because they have so much to do in terms of working out, meditating, journaling, taking care of themselves and the kids, eating well, running a successful business, going on date night with their husbands and being generally overall fabulous, and if you don't do all this, you don't add up,' Nidhi says.

This perfection trap follows women to work too, where they are expected to be likable and agreeable rather than ambitious. Men are ambitious, women are aggressive. Men look focused when they are frowning, women should smile more. A Northwestern University analysis looked into how gender stereotypes in the US have evolved over seven decades (1946–2018), in which over 30,000 people found that while women were viewed as more competent than men, men were still viewed as more ambitious, aggressive and decisive than women. Women were viewed as 'more compassionate, affectionate and sensitive than men,' which affects how they are viewed as leaders, which is often synonymous with aggressive ambition.[7]

Studies have established beyond doubt that while men are rewarded for expressing anger, women are penalized for it. Women often face the 'double-bind' or 'assertiveness penalty' (when they are assertive, they are less liked) at work. According to researchers, when women were perceived to be aggressive at work, their pay dropped by 35 per cent while the same aggressive behaviour in men only led to a 17.5 per cent decrease, underlining how identical behaviours are judged and penalized differently based on gender. An article titled 'Gender Bias at Work: The Assertiveness Double-Bind' says that for women, 'likability can be an even more important factor than competence for getting hired and women who breach gender stereotypes may jeopardize their career prospects.'[8]

Women as leaders is a concession made by patriarchy and hence, women must stay within those set boundaries—they must smile more, look pretty and be agreeable—because their promotion is dependent on a system created by men. The moment those traits of the perfect 'woman worker' are breached, women are penalized for it. Women can be labelled as bossy just for asking for a promotion or a raise, no matter how well-deserved it is.

According to the article, 'Women receive "negative personality criticism", such as being called bossy or told to "watch their tone" in around 75 per cent of performance reviews. Men, on the other hand, rarely do. Women receive 2.5 times the amount of feedback men do about aggressive communication styles, with phrases such as "Your speaking style is off-putting." Women are described as being "abrasive" far more often than men."[9]

Is it any wonder then that women feel compelled to play to the gender stereotypes that have been predetermined for their economic empowerment?

Very few women are directly aggressive—preferring to dial it down in situations of conflict and being passive-aggressive instead. For years, I described my leadership style as collaborative. And how has that worked for me? The men, even the younger ones, have walked all over me while the women have nodded their heads vigorously but gone about their own way. After a bitter experience a few years ago, I realized that thanks to male-dominated workplaces, there was only one leadership style—abrasive, aggressive, manipulative and exploitative, and unnecessary optics such as talking unnecessarily in meetings or hanging around at work beyond work hours. I think men have too much time on their hands—it is time to get them to share caregiving and keep them robustly occupied as they want to be. After my own bitter experience,

I swore off being in leadership positions (I am not alone—many women have stepped down from high positions because they could not align their leadership style to that of the organization—because it is a system set up to fail women). I have been a consultant since and have never been happier. I still am in a leading position but I am firmer now and more direct. But in the back of my mind, the fight or fly mode is always on. This is a kind of workplace trauma many women carry with them.

'I still need to work on my aggression. I give you an example from the conversation I just had before speaking to you. There is a colleague from the business network, who called me up yesterday when I was in the middle of a business meeting—on a coaching call, actually. It was a call, which rang a number of times and, of course, I did not pick it up as I was mid-session. There was no accompanying or following message. I got busy with my work and I did not follow up,' Nidhi says. 'When I called back the next day, he was trying his best to make me feel guilty for not prioritizing his unscheduled call. I was furious because I stuck to my schedule and called him when my schedule permitted. Even though I dialled down the situation and explained why I couldn't call him back, I don't think I made my point that strongly. Or maybe I am judging myself too harshly. A man in my place would have been firmer, pointing out the randomness of his call and their packed schedule.'

Nidhi keeps second-guessing herself even when it comes to what she says—a legacy of the perfection trap. We have already been given a script for how to act when we are at home or work, and the moment we veer from the script, it's uncomfortable for everyone. That's exactly why we must scrunch up that list in our heads and do what suits us the best. We don't need to be like the male leaders or professionals—we need to lead like our individual personalities allow us to. Throw away all those leadership books—they are not meant for women; they are meant to train women as substitutes for men. The idea of the systems we have—at home, in the workplace—is to keep women dependent on men.

Women must cater to a certain image of the woman worker—smiley, agreeable, non-aggressive—otherwise, as the stats above show, they can be penalized for deviating from that image.

'There is a difference between the leadership style of a man and a woman because their temperaments are vastly different. The difference between the feminine and masculine energies is a beautiful one. It's not something you should be ashamed of. Most women are softer, kinder and more compassionate, and that is exactly why we make excellent leaders,' says Dr Yadav.

'Women are good team leaders,' she adds, because 'they take the team along and are more collaborative. Women are often non-confrontational because our patriarchal society has fixed the image of the 'good girl/woman' as one who is compliant and docile. We have to work on ourselves, identify the limiting beliefs that are holding us back and learn the skill of assertiveness.

And it is a skill that can be learnt and perfected if you work on it.'

'Start by being assertive at home,' Dr Yadav advises. 'And then start saying "no" more. Those are the skills we need to learn, practice and then implement. But, having said that, women don't need to be assertive like men—they should be assertive in their own way that keeps them comfortable.'

That is a very important distinction. What is a man's assertiveness? Being loud, rude and in your face. Many men I have met over the course of my life and work love to say, 'I say what I have to say to your face.' But then, they also go behind your back and say some more. I might be wrong, but for most men, hypocrisy is a way of life. Most are so full of themselves that they hold themselves up as the ideal and have really messed up the real definition of a true leader—one who is collaborative, kind, understanding and empathetic. And that's how women lead. That's how I have always led—firm but not brash, assertive but not rude, inclusive and not arrogant, empathetic and not pretentious. There are also many men who lead like that—I have worked under some of them and my husband is one among them. But a majority have completely corrupted the idea of a leader.

I decided some years earlier that I do not need to go out of my way to be 'nice' or 'likeable' at work—that it is the definition of a 'perfect woman employee' and it is a male construct. Things became harder and there was much more resistance, but I persisted. I remember a meeting sometime in 2020 when I interrupted my male colleagues who would constantly talk over me in meetings—I was loud and I was clear. There was actually a split second of silence while the men recovered from the shock of me not being a soft-spoken colleague. I am not ashamed to admit that my heart beat that much faster as I made my point loudly and clearly, taking the lead and letting them know that out of all of them present in that meeting, I was the only expert. Yes, my heart thudded loudly and my throat ran dry, but I knew I needed to do it. It comes naturally to me now but the first time is always the hardest. And just imagine how long it took me to reach here—2020 was just four years ago and I had played into the perfection trap for eighteen years and more if I take into account the emotional and physical expectations. So, it's never too late to break the perfection trap.

Women also put in way too much effort at work to prove they are worth probably a quarter of the returns they bring.

'I never realized this but I was trying way harder than men to prove at work that I was good. It didn't register at that time but when I look back now, I realize that I was putting in so much more effort than my male colleagues. And it was because my confidence was so low that I just never would believe that I was as good or better,' says Priya.

Men are assertive but women are aggressive, men are ambitious but women are pushy or bossy, men have passion, women have hysterics, what is determination in men is just stubbornness in a woman and the best of the lot—men are persistent and persuasive but women are—you got it—nagging. These stereotypes follow women around in their personal and professional lives, affecting their self-worth and self-image and pushing them to be more perfect than is required.

Women are not considered natural leaders because of the perception of leadership being a 'tough' job whereas women must be always sweetness and light with a twinkle in their eyes and a bounce in their steps. Women are always treading the thin line between the roles of both 'woman' and 'leader'.

Women in Science, Technology, Engineering and Math (STEM) have the additional burden of proving that they have as much of a 'math brain' as their male colleagues. Men are not naturally good at math but girls are discriminated against when it comes to studying science and math—just like the way they are kept away from high growth better-paid jobs in manufacturing and engineering while being pushed towards so-called 'feminine' jobs like teaching or beauty and lifestyle.

As Bardoloi had said in the first chapter—we are the first generation who are making the connections, calling things out and trying to reset the course. The women I came across during the writing of this book—from the ones in their mid-twenties to ones in their fifties—were connecting the dots, too. They are embracing their imperfections and cutting themselves some much-needed slack.

'I set the standards very high for my own self, both at work and home. If I have to give 2–3 options for something, I will give five. If something needs to be done by Wednesday, it will be done by Monday. I think it's because I constantly feel the need to prove my worth,' an acquaintance told me.

Perfection is subjective—what is perfect to you might be imperfect to someone else.

'Apart from my family members (that too, not all) and a few close friends, I ignore what others say or think about me. I just focus on the work/responsibility at hand, give my best and leave the outcome to be what it will be. Of course, I've reached this stage after years of hurt and heartbreak. I've developed a thick skin (at least outwardly). I keep reminding myself that I'm not perfect and that's normal because no one is perfect,' a young woman I interviewed told me.

To me, it is crystal clear now that I will never be good enough for everybody—so I will just be good enough for myself.

'I don't think perfectionism is an easy beast to tame because it is the side effect of something deeper. People want to be perfectionists when they are unsure of themselves or insecure. So, there are good days and bad. But every time you're doing something and you have to present it to the world, it creeps back in; or every time you're even being a mother to your child, it just creeps back in. So, to constantly think that you need to be better because you're never good enough, that is a beast that is very difficult to tame,' a close friend told me once during our many conversations about life.

'But I am always very conscious. When I see it getting too much, I consciously take a step back and re-evaluate. The acceptance of what is enough for you as a person is very important. And you are the only one who can decide that.'

My friend, however, feels that our generation is judged less harshly than our mother's generation. I am not sure if that is entirely true—even if there is no overt or direct judgement, a lot of indirect or silent reproaches for not being perfect can be felt. Women can sense this judgement, and often, quite keenly. And yes, we do overthink, but then that's how we have been socialized. If a woman prioritizes her work over her child, for example, there are invisible voices in her head telling her that she is doing something wrong. And while the voices might be invisible, they are not imaginary. They are there because they are a part of her lived experiences.

'When I was a new mother, every time the baby cried, I took it as a personal failure. The only way to deal with it was to remind myself that perfection is a myth and that doing my best is good enough. I now tell this to younger women,' says Natasha.

The perfect mother trope comes right on the heels of the other perfection trap—that of the domestic goddess. Studies have shown that women are judged more harshly than men for not keeping a flawless home. Whether men are immune to mess or they just can't be bothered is a discussion for another day, but the fact that they can't see mess (although studies have proved that is not true—men and women see mess the same way) is owing to the fact that they are not held responsible for it but women are.

Housework has a gender, and it's female. I remember so many times at friends' houses—watching them rush around trying to clean the house while also fixing everyone's meals and checking their watches so as not to be late for work. I do it myself. I have seen my mother not having time to make her own lunch box but never leaving the home without it looking spic and span. She always told my sister and me, 'Never leave a dirty house behind—you won't like it when you come back.' Even if this is true, it hides a bitter truth that if women won't clean the house, then it won't be cleaned at all. Once I asked a friend of mine about why we do this. Her reply was simple. 'I can't leave the home in such a mess. If someone walks in, they will blame me for being careless and untidy.' Sadly, she was right.

Nidhi remembers the time when she had once sent a picture taken in her backyard to her sister, and the yard was unkempt. 'My sister said she was surprised at the state of my backyard as she thought I was very efficient,' Nidhi says. 'That's how everyone thinks. I mean I sent a happy picture of myself and my child, and all she sees is my messy backyard.'

In 2015, an article in the *Guardian* pointed out that some studies had found differences in communication styles, suggesting that more women tend to exhibit passive-aggressive behaviour compared to men.[10] However, it's important to emphasize that this observation does not imply that women are inherently more calculating or devious. Rather, it can be attributed to the broader context of power dynamics.

The article noted that women often find themselves in positions of lower power, especially in workplace settings where assertiveness can sometimes lead to negative consequences for them. In such situations, the passive-aggressive approach may become a more frequently utilized communication strategy among women as a means of navigating these power dynamics.

But often, when women are ambitious, they imbibe what are essentially male leadership traits, and because they are still trying to fit in, instead of following the leadership style that comes naturally to them, they are harsher with women while seeking validation from men. As talked about earlier, many women leave leadership positions because they are unable to exercise the leadership styles they are comfortable with. When I tried to use my own empathetic leadership style at my last job, I was humiliated, harassed and exploited (by women as well as male co-workers) because I came across as 'weak' when I was being empathetic and refused to lead like a man by terrorizing the employees. I walked out of that job but I still carry the scars that have made me stay away from leadership positions ever since because it's not worth my peace of mind. Leadership, like every other toxic workplace trait, is a male construct that still believes in that archaic concept of 'survival of the fittest'.

'Women definitely need to evaluate how to become tough bosses without becoming replicas of toxic masculinity,' says Dipsikha. 'I gave up trying to find that elusive sweet spot where I could harness my soft skills and still command loyalty and get things done, which is why l left advertising and joined a very lean, flat, unconventional Israeli diamond company. It was the best professional decision I took after nine years in advertising.'

Women routinely diminish themselves at work which manifests as self-doubt and imposter syndrome. In my conversations with women, the imposter syndrome came up over and over again.

First talked about in the 1970s, imposter syndrome can be loosely defined as a behavioural health phenomenon that people go through when they feel like they're not as smart or capable as others think they are. Psychologists Pauline Rose Clance and Suzanne Imes were the first to study this in 1978. They found that even though women were doing really well in school or at work, they still felt like they were tricking people into believing they were smart.

A 2022 report by KPMG, *Advancing the Future of Women in Business: A KPMG Women's Leadership Summit Report*, found that 75 per cent of executive women experienced imposter syndrome at certain points in their careers and 81 per cent believed they were working harder than men to not fail.[11]

But this syndrome spells trouble for women—it makes them think that if they do everything perfectly, no one will realize they feel unsure about their abilities.

After working as a journalist for over two decades, I still struggle with the question—'Is this all a fluke? Am I just an imposter?' After my first book was published, I was almost fatalistic in my expectation that someone would call me out for being an imposter—any positive review I received was not enough to make me feel like I deserved those accolades; that I had trudged a long way battling several discriminations, sexual harassment, attempts by male colleagues to diminish me or to block me out from newsrooms. That I still made it. I am still standing strong. I am still able to not just tell my story but the stories of other women. And yet, do I completely believe that I am enough, that I am not an imposter? I don't know. I honestly don't know. There could be the smallest trigger for me to feel that I am a nobody, a nothing.

When I asked my women interviewees if they ever felt like an imposter, it touched a raw nerve. Every woman I spoke to told me about their struggle with it. One woman had started a Formula 1 column in 2021, but every time she wrote and published, she dreaded that someone would come along and point out that she didn't understand the sport and should 'shut up'. Someone got selected for a fellowship and was convinced that she qualified because of the organization she represented and not her own experience or qualifications. Another person backs out of applying for jobs whose criteria she fits if it mentions phrases like 'self-starter, critical thinker, innovator.' And then, there is the personal imposter syndrome. My mother, whenever she calls me or anyone else for that matter, is always so apologetic that she is imposing on their time as if she is not important enough for the person to spend time talking to her. 'I don't make just checking-on-you or touching-base calls to friends or family because I don't think any of them would want to hear from me. Also, I don't tweet much because who would want to hear my opinion?' one of my interviewees told me.

'I am a case study in self-doubt and imposter syndrome,' one woman told me, immediately apologizing for the rant.

'I am smarter and more articulate than most other people I know but believe me, I am cringing so much just vocalizing this,' another woman told me.

At work, especially, the imposter syndrome is holding women back from really pushing through. 'I don't push myself forward for a role, presuming that my work will speak for itself. What I never realized is that even if my work speaks, my silence indicates a lack of interest. How do I address this?' another young woman asked me during our conversation.

Women rarely speak about their work or their achievements, but in doing so, they allow others to steal their work and their ideas—all because they are just not sure if they are capable enough. And society has done nothing to boost women's confidence either.

I always feel that whatever I have achieved has been a stroke of luck—a turn of fate. But the older I get, the more I realize that there is nothing called a turn of fate. What we achieve is what we set our minds to. And for women, it takes double the work to achieve their dreams and aspirations. I still cannot talk about my work—every time I publish something and despite doing this regularly for two decades, I am still uncertain for days after publication and feel like I have somehow gotten some important details wrong. It is my imposter syndrome that makes me sweat over the simple emails or text messages, and it's a constant battle.

Other women had similar stories of doubting their capabilities, attributing their successes to luck or chance, despite being hardworking, sincere and talented.

Another young woman I spoke to said that she recently defended her PhD thesis 'and while it is tradition (at least in European universities) for friends and family to attend, I told everyone to stay away. I just don't want anyone I know to read my work or listen to me talk about it because I think they will realize that it's not that great. Having grown up in an environment where all my validation comes from grades/work/achievements, I am very paranoid about people thinking I am "not smart".'

I was quite surprised when I started talking to women about self-perception and confidence in oneself, and many said they hated the first time they heard themselves on audio or saw themselves in a video. Why was I surprised? Because I thought I was the only one. The first time I heard myself on the radio, I closed my eyes in embarrassment. The same happened when I first saw myself on video. But since then, I have constantly challenged and pushed myself to step out of the box and do things that embarrass or terrify me, because I have realized that this embarrassment, this fear, is also an important part of the social conditioning of women. Faces change, but stories remain the same. 'Lately, I have been challenging myself to step out of my comfort zone and do things that make me feel less "safe". I am doing this because I think it's important to push ourselves out of the box into areas we want to grow into,' one interviewee told me.

'I do a lot of affirmations where I reflect on my achievements and my strengths. I no longer feel intimidated in large group settings where I am the only woman who might also be leading that discussion,' said another.

Once, when Hilary Clinton was asked for some advice for young working women at Tina Brown's 'Women in the World' conference in New York, a notable event that focuses on women's issues and empowerment, she famously said, 'At this point in my career, I've employed so many young people. One of the differences I saw is that when I say to a young woman, "I want you to take on this extra responsibility," almost invariably she says, "Do you think I'm ready?" But when I ask a man, he goes, "How high, how fast, when do I start?"'[12]

Twelve years ago, Natasha was recruiting for an associate for which she had specified a minimum of three years of relevant experience. A young woman with two and a half years of experience had applied and mentioned in her cover letter that even though she had two and half years of experience, she really wanted to apply for the job. She added that if not now, then she would like to apply when she completes three years of experience. 'But at the end of the interview, I kind of knew I was taking her on because she was really good. She had not even been keen to apply (due to her experience being less) but her partner had forced her to. Many men would confidently apply with less experience, but women must be 100 per cent sure they match the requirements of a job before they apply.'

'I would tell young girls to go for that dream job even if they don't match 100 per cent. Write a cover letter explaining you don't match completely and then outline the reasons why they should still call you for an interview,' she adds.

But wanting to be perfect also has its roots in approval, especially male approval. Women have spent so much of their lives trying to win approval for what they want to do—even something as basic as living their lives, doing their jobs or simply minding their own business—that this has become second nature to them. And this is where it becomes complicated.

The conditioning that women are subjected to right from birth tells them that the whole premise of their life must be based on unconditional love and yet, they cannot complain if that love is not returned. Many women go through life convinced that they are not worthy of being loved. It breaks my heart when I speak to these women—and there are just too many of them—who believe that they do not have the love they deserve because they are unworthy. This, in turn, traps them into this idea of perfection, underlying which is the need to be loved by the one who 'provides' (the man).

But once you identify this trap, you can free yourself. The first thing to remember is that perfectionism is a myth—no one is perfect, no one needs to be perfect and the definition varies from one person to another. Something that has so many variables is, at best, an imagined concept and at worst, a form of manipulation. Every stage of my life that I have now left behind appears perfect to me and yet, while I was in that stage, I was unhappy and dissatisfied. That feels to me to be such a waste—one that I never want to repeat. Recently, I came across this post on LinkedIn by author and shame researcher Brene Brown where she called perfectionism an 'armour' based on the belief that 'if we do things perfectly and look perfect, we can minimize or avoid the pain of blame, judgment and shame.'[13]

'Perfectionism,' she says, 'is not the key to success. In fact, it hampers achievement as it is correlated with depression, anxiety, addiction, and life paralysis or missed opportunities. The fear of failing, making mistakes, not meeting people's expectations and being criticized keeps us outside of the arena where healthy competition and striving unfolds. Perfectionism is a twenty-ton shield that we lug around, thinking it will protect us, when in fact it's the thing that's really preventing us from being seen.'

The myth of perfection in women is driven by a sense of shame—shame that we are not enough, that we are not good or great or even passable sometimes. This shame is something, especially in the Indian context, that is handed down as a trauma from the moment a girl is born. We are born with the shame of being unwanted, and if not unwanted, then the shame of trying to make sure that we honour that and so on.

Perfection cannot be the end goal of your life—instead, focus on your effort and progress. Don't compare your achievements with others—they have different stories than you. Failure is essential in life as it makes your journey and experiences complete. There's always so much more to learn—and if there's no end to learning, then it makes the idea of anything perfect void. Reconcile what you know with how you feel—that's the key to an informed life.

'I allow myself to fail spectacularly. I refuse to be perfect. And my loved ones have now accepted me for who I am,' says Nidhi. 'I didn't give them a choice.'

Nidhi tells her daughter to prioritize her own happiness over societal expectations. 'There is a lot of peer pressure,' she says. 'But I am teaching her to align her achievements with her happiness. Perfection is a myth. Just being aware of yourself and remembering who you are is most important and as long as you are trying, it's okay.'

Mridvika, too, escaped the perfection trap quite recently. 'I wanted to be a perfect mother and a super-ambitious entrepreneur. But right now, I feel perfection is just the enemy of completion. I think, there will come a point in your life when you will realize that being done is better than being perfect,' she says. 'And yes, I went through the usual emotions of being disappointed in myself and asking myself if I was losing my ambitions, but I also did not want to wake up any more while a mountain of things remained to be done. So, it was what it was. I can't function any more on three to four hours of sleep, I need at least six to seven. So, I failed and then I got up and readjusted the lens through which I was looking at life.'

'You have to look good for the men because we are always catering to the male gaze no matter how woke we are. The need to be approved by the male gaze is so much so that women abandon themselves. We are conditioned so much and unconditioning takes a lifetime. It's such a dangerous trap,' Bardoloi says. 'This is the hardest trap to ever come out of. I have worked on myself for 10–15 years to come out of it. Have I personally come out of the trap completely? No. I am still working on myself. It will take one more generation to start chipping away at it because we live in a system that respects and honours the way things are. "Look, she is a teacher and a mother of four, and she still comes home and serves tea to everyone." That is what is celebrated.'

'Your self-perception can significantly influence how you behave in a relationship. This can affect various aspects, including intimacy, and even your sex drive, especially after having children. I'm trying to be open and honest here. There are times when I feel that my husband might have certain expectations about how I should look, and these expectations can sometimes be overwhelming,' says Mridvika. Mridvika raises an important point—this stress on perfection, especially in terms of one's looks, can negatively impact spousal relationships.

Sometimes, we trap ourselves in this hell hole. Mridvika has curly hair and when she ties them in a bun, the baby hair on her forehead stands up all frizzy. 'My husband always says, "What have you done to your hair?" and it never fails to make me conscious. He doesn't mean "I hate you because of what you have done to your hair" but to me, it says something about my appearance—so much so that I started looking for solutions to tame baby hair. I have already spent a fortune to buy products I didn't need. It was just one offhand comment that he casually threw while walking past me, and it got me spiralling. My learning from that was that I have to stop trying to fit into some mould the moment someone comments on my appearance. It's just baby hair for God's sake,' she laughs.

It's 2024 and we have still not busted the myth of the *perfect woman* or redefined it. A perfect woman is not someone who excels as a domestic goddess and a career diva, or someone who fits into the socially prescribed mould of existing—a perfect woman is one who is happy and fulfilled, at peace with herself, knows where to draw the line, and is not moving through life worried, stressed, harried, feeling suicidal, underappreciated or unacknowledged. A perfect woman is someone who sleeps soundly at night, whose smile reaches her eyes and who feels free.

In their influential study conducted nearly thirty years ago, academics Gordon Flett and Paul Hewitt, highly regarded experts in the field of perfectionism, identified the three primary dimensions of perfectionism. These were 'self-oriented perfectionism', which pertains to the pursuit of high personal standards and self-critical tendencies; 'other-oriented perfectionism,' which involves placing excessively high expectations on others; and 'socially prescribed perfectionism,' which is quite self-explanatory—standards of perfection set by society.[14] In a woman's life, it is the third that leads them to the first two and together, the effects are exhausting. These expectations of perfection lead many women to anxiety, depression, and thoughts of self-harm.

It is here that the body positivity movement has helped many women. Research shows that the movement began to gain ground on Instagram around 2012 and generated a total of thirteen million social media posts till 2020.[15]

According to a 2019 study, body positivity challenges stereotypes about physical appearances and encourages acceptance of oneself with all of one's so-called 'shortcomings'.[16]

Then there's also body neutrality, which I find more empowering. While body positivity centres on the belief that all bodies are beautiful, body neutrality looks at bodies as functional things. It takes the focus away from traditional body standards and rejects the notion that self-worth is tied to appearance. No one can constantly feel positive about anything, and why should that be any different from the way we look at our bodies? We need to think of our bodies in a neutral manner and not give them the power to make or break us. A body is just anatomy—at the end of the day, it is just skin, bones, fat and muscles. Can we really let that decide who we become in our minds?

Maybe we can break free when we focus on who we are inside rather than what's on the outside. M, for example, was trapped in a man's body for many years of her life. She was expected to be a man, but her soul was that of a woman. She was a woman. And if she had focused on the outside rather than who she was inside, she would still be trapped in the man's body she was born with. There's such a great lesson to learn from her experience—listening to our inner voice, the person we know we are, and not getting lost in the definition imposed on us by other circumstances. 'I am standing alone as a mountain. Winds collide with me to produce rain. It is a capability of the winds or maybe my ruthlessness. I have kept alive the strength within me. The earth is a woman, who else has powers to accept and retain like the earth?' she says.

M, who adores Rabindranath Tagore, quoted him often during our conversations. 'Listen to this,' she told me. '"*Ninda porbo bhushan kore, kaatar konthohaar, mathay kore tule lobo opomaaner bhaar*" (I'll wear criticism as my attire and as a thorny necklace, and will bear my insults on the head), so he is turning the negatives into positives. "*Aashbe pothe aandhar neme, tai bole ki roibi theme, tui baare baare jalbi baati, hoyto baati jolbena, apon loke chharbe toke, ta bole, bhabna kora cholbena*" (Roads will be inflicted with darkness, will you not move? Light up a lamp, maybe it won't light up, your own may leave you, but worry you must not). Did Tagore know that these lines would be so appropriate for trans people?'

Or to women, too?

And then she broke into a Tagore song that made my eyes well up.

Mabhoi baanir bhorsa niye, chhera paal bhuk bhoriye . . .
Poth amar shei dekhabe je amare chay, ami obhoy mone chharbo tori, Ei sudhu mor daye go . . .

'In the song, the poet is sailing in a boat with a broken sail. How can one take a boat out with a broken sail? Every part has something negative, but he is turning them into positives. Tagore writes, "Notwithstanding all the difficulties thrown my way, I'll surely reach you,"' M explained.*

The analogy is so beautiful that I stayed with it for a long while after our conversation ended. And through her lens, I could see what women could be if they had been allowed to just be. I also remembered how my childhood was replete with my mother reciting Tagore's poetry to me—she also took great strength as well as many life lessons in how to let go and think positively, given the constraints of her life.

Self-love is the only way to end this vicious cycle of endless perfection that is imposed on women across societies and cultures. Somewhere along the way, women have forgotten how to love themselves because they have been so busy teaching themselves to love everyone else. Cisgender-heterosexual women (women whose gender identity matches their birth sex and are attracted to the opposite sex) have certain societal privileges. However, these same privileges can

* This song is from *Gitabitan*, a collection of all 2232 songs written by Rabindranath Tagore.

be limiting as well because of the societal expectations tied to them, which restricts their experiences and self-perception. We need to look at women's experiences through an inclusive and intersectional lens. This means considering how different aspects of a woman's identity (like her caste, sexual orientation, gender identity, etc.) overlap and affect her life. When we consider women who face more marginalization due to their caste, sexual orientation, gender identity, etc., the concept of self-love becomes clearer because the challenges and barriers it has to face are more pronounced in these groups, offering a starker contrast to the idea of always putting others first.

'I loved myself so much that I never wanted to dim my soul. My soul was at peace the day I started the process of becoming a woman. I cannot explain the feeling,' says Nitasha, who was born a boy in a middle-class family in Kolkata. When she finally decided to transition to a woman, she found herself alone. 'My journey was hard. If I didn't love myself, I would not have stayed the course and we would not be talking today. When you love yourself, you become the best version of yourself, and that is a gift. Being a woman is a blessing despite all the challenges—it's euphoric. This is why we must love ourselves, take care of ourselves—physically and mentally—and most importantly, appreciate ourselves. Because if we don't, others won't either.'

Women can teach each other so much if only we were able to come together in communities and support groups and share our experiences—not theoretical, bookish knowledge—but raw, unfiltered lived experiences. When I first spoke to M and Nitasha, I told them that I wanted to learn from their experiences and journeys because often, we get so caught up in our struggles that we lose sight of what is important. As Dr Yadav constantly points out, feminine energy is beautiful and different and we really should not lose sight of that. And when we look at womanhood from the eyes of M or Nitasha, it looks beautiful—as it should be. To be a woman and to take pride in being a woman is the first step to self-discovery, self-worth, self-love and the ability to redefine everything that has been fed to us as the reality of our existence, which is nothing but patriarchal propaganda. The first time I spoke to M, I came away with this beautiful thought that she had said: 'I had to love myself because no one else was willing to.'

I then realized that I had to learn to love myself because every other love seemed to be transactional or conditional (consciously or unconsciously).

I remember now what a wise and highly accomplished woman had once told me—'I don't want to be perfect; I want to be happy, successful and retire rich with all my broken pieces.'

5

The Guilt Factory

> 'There are two kinds of guilt. The kind that's a burden and the kind that gives you purpose. Let your guilt be your fuel. Let it remind you of who you want to be. Draw a line in your mind. Never cross it again. You have a soul. It's damaged but it's there. Don't let them take it from you.'
>
> —Sabaa Tahir

An angelic smile lit up his cutely puckered face as he sucked contentedly on the pacifier, but guilt was coursing through me as I watched him from afar while chewing my thumb.

It was 2005 and I was a new mother to a three-month-old. My son was a night owl.

It all started a couple of weeks earlier when I just couldn't take the strain of staying up all night any more.

I was walking around like a zombie struggling to finish my work during the day when I came across an article about using pacifiers to calm babies. The pacifier was bought and put in the baby's mouth. And the peace that followed it—bliss. I slept for the first time in two months and subsequently felt immense guilt that I might have hooked my baby to something addictive.

But from the next month, advice started pouring in from people who were neither doctors nor had any connection with the medical profession—'Don't give him the pacifier, it is a bad habit', 'You must take him off it when he is three months old' or 'The shape of his lips or his front teeth will be spoiled.' And from there started the guilt trip—every time I put the pacifier in my baby's mouth, I felt guilty. Was I being selfish for just a night's sleep? By the end of the week, I was convinced I was a bad mother.

I argued for and against the pacifier in my own head while mashing his food, making myself a sandwich or taking a shower. I started reducing the time of the pacifier and then just stopped giving it to him altogether. After two weeks, the pacifier had been thrown out. For years after, when Che had these adorable bunny-like front teeth, in my mind I was wracked with guilt that one week of a pacifier must have ruined his teeth. Guilt is the bane of a woman's existence. She cannot escape it. We go through life battling various guilts but the most consuming one for women is the caregiving guilt which includes a mother's and daughter's guilt.

'Sometimes when I look at my kids going through different phases, I feel guilty and responsible—that somehow I am not doing enough, that somehow I am causing it,' says Nidhi.

But she had to deal with her mother's guilt—she told me she had to as there was no other choice. 'After struggling with this compulsion of trying to be the perfect mother to my children, I have come to the realization that nothing is in my control. What is in my control is the fact that I show up every day to care for my children with the best possible intentions. I don't worry about the outcomes any more.'

Some years ago, I had accompanied an all-women expedition team of environmental scientists, engineers and biologists studying plastic pollution in the Ganges to better understand and document how plastic waste travels to the oceans and fill critical knowledge gaps.

The group's scientists were from all over the world—the United States, the United Kingdom, Australia, India, Bangladesh and so on. They were all experts of international repute in their chosen fields and came from different societies—some were more permissive of women's rights whereas others were not, yet there was something they all had in common.

The mommy guilt.

I often caught the women sneaking in a few minutes to call home, talk to their children and motivate them for their school tests. Most of them had to stay away from their families for months on end but they were always trying to negotiate some time to fly back home without compromising their research. 'It's my son's eleventh birthday soon . . . I will fly home then for a few days,' one of them told me, straining to be heard above the roar of the motor dinghy and the river breeze that carried her words over the filthy water.

'The "mommy guilt" is deeply embedded in our society. And we are made to feel that if we are not around our kids constantly, we are not "good" mothers,' another one of the women scientists told me.

'I have a growing daughter,' one of the Bangladeshi scientists had told me. When she travels, she calls her daughter three times a day, her husband once every night while also being in touch with her daughter's school to monitor her schoolwork.

Studies have shown how working mothers often feel more guilty than working dads. Usually, after having a baby, moms tend to work outside less and do more at home, while dads keep working the same or more. Age-old ideas about who should work (men) and who should provide care (women) become the cause of unfairness at work and at home. For example, working moms might get less interesting work or have trouble moving up in their careers because they also have to focus on their families. On the other hand, dads who help out a lot at home might be seen as not manly, and moms who focus on work might be called cold or selfish. These expectations usually make moms cut back on work to take care of the house more.[1]

I've always had an issue with how we put motherhood on a pedestal and the huge pressure it puts on women. There's pressure to have kids, to be perfect moms who give up everything for their kids, and finally, to deal with feeling lost when the kids leave home. It feels like women just can't win. As a mom, I always felt like I was being judged by some invisible audience, where one small mistake could make me a 'bad mother'. It took me years to realize that being empathetic and compassionate was enough. I had a strained relationship with my mother while growing up because she was so strict. It was only later that I realized that her constant worry and anxieties were not so much about me but about her own perceived shortcomings. Because she chose to work instead of staying home, there were people who were always insinuating that she was not doing enough for her children. Growing up, I saw my dad as the fun, kind parent and my mom as the strict one. But this is just how society conditions us to see parents. The dad is often seen as the hero who saves us from mom's scolding, but he's only called in when things get serious.

Dads are like fun guests who bring joy, kind of like Santa Claus. While moms do the everyday work of raising kids, it is the dads who are seen bringing fun, much like Santa with his once-a-year gifts. It sometimes feels like kids value what dads do more even though moms are working hard all the time.

And just like we glorify the idea of a superwoman to hide how much unpaid caregiving women do, we also glorify motherhood to trap women into thinking they have to be saints and sacrifice everything for their kids. And if they ever complain, they're labelled 'bad moms'. We don't need labels like 'supermom' or 'superwoman'. Also, did you notice that there are no 'super dads', and 'superman' is just a fictional character?

'Should motherhood really be glorified as much as it is? There are so many people who desire to become parents and realize it is different from what they think. Not everyone is designed to be a parent; it requires a lot of effort,' says Nidhi. 'It's high time we demystify motherhood. The pressure to have children and the associated mother's guilt are crazy. Sometimes, people end up having kids because of this pressure or because of this glorification of motherhood. Even when women are well-educated and enlightened, they still succumb to this socialization consciously or unconsciously.'

For Natasha, her understanding of motherhood and the guilt it carried along with it, changed substantially after she had her second child. 'I did not feel as inadequate as I did before. If I was a horrible mother, I was okay with it because who really set the bar?' But she was conscious of this more than she would like to admit and would often apologize to her kids for not being the perfect mother. But her kids set her straight. 'They always were firm and told me they liked me for who I am and would like to help me in every way I needed them to.'

Who really decides who is the most important parent in terms of a child's upbringing? Isn't it time to stop pushing these gender roles on our children—play football with their fathers and run to their mothers when they fall and scrape their knees? Sounds familiar, right? We have been fed this image of the demarcation of parenthood—actually, the role of women as mothers—so much and for so long that it's become an internalized emotion.

Natasha says, 'I realized that there was no right or wrong way to be a mother. Children only respond to love. I do suffer from mother's guilt from time to time but I have realized my sons have been brought up differently and they love me and I am proud of them. I have to stop worrying about being a horrible mother or a bad parent. Every mother is different and does her best in every way that is possible for them.'

Natasha has worked out a way that works for her children, her partner and herself. 'In our family, my husband acts as a traditional mother and not me. If there is an emergency, he's the one to take care of the situation,' she says. 'People will still point fingers and say, "But as a mother, you were not there"—and to that I say, mothers don't need to be there all the time.'

It's a part of our unlearning process—this social construct of the 'mother' as a superhuman caregiver; whose own care needs require no attention because 'she can manage' or 'she always manages'. The cape doesn't allow us to fly, it shackles us down.

The social construct of a 'mother' is the way society defines and expects individuals who identify as female or are biologically female, to fulfil particular roles and responsibilities related to parenting and caregiving. This construct includes various cultural and societal expectations, norms and values regarding motherhood. Key elements include mothers being viewed as primary caregivers responsible for their children's well-being (traditional gender roles often designate women as primary caregivers), the expectation of strong emotional bonds between mothers and children, the idea that mothers should be selfless and willing to sacrifice personal needs, and the assumption that they should also take on a significant share of household duties. Additionally, societal stereotypes and expectations often portray mothers as nurturing and patient, and they may face judgment and criticism related to their parenting choices and abilities.

As sociologists have at various times pointed out, 'The confusions of biological and cultural predispositions of men and women to parenting are grounded in a broader system of gender inequalities.' Katarzyna Suwada, in her study, 'Parenting, Gender and Work: A Sociological Perspective', found that while the family was 'one of the most important and the most resilient of social institutions,' it was also 'one of the most gendered ones' which means that it functioned on the foundation of 'gender roles and unequal gender relations'.[2]

A 2022 study titled 'Mothering Ideology: A Qualitative Exploration of Mothers' Perceptions of Navigating Motherhood Pressures and Partner Relationships', talked about the 'good mother ideology' and how subscribing to it 'is associated with conforming to traditional gender roles, which impacts how mothers navigate their partner's involvement in child-rearing and contributes to a change in their identity as a partner after becoming a mother'.

'Good mother ideology refers to beliefs that women are only "good" mothers if they adhere to the tenets of dominant parenting discourse, such as intensive mothering ideology, which prioritizes children's needs and child-raising above all else,' the study found. 'Undergirded by this ideology, mothers' attempts to navigate the transition to motherhood are fraught with pressures, and the transition is associated with negative health outcomes for mothers and children.'[3]

'I have accepted the fact that I cannot be perfect all the time and something has to be dropped somewhere. I realized this relatively early when my kids were very young,' says Natasha. 'I do know people whose kids are in college and they are still struggling to be perfect parents. I realized relatively early that I cannot be perfect and that I should just do what I can.'

In my conversations with women of my age—early to mid-forties—I have found them to be accepting of this guilt, but also actively addressing it. They are adamant not to pass it down to the next generation, especially to their daughters. I have made peace with the fact that I cannot be solely responsible for providing care and that my partner was equally able. In fact, after many years, I can accept that Bau, my partner, is actually a much better parent to our son and our two canine babies than I am, because, on most days, I am a mess when he is emotionally more patient and present. As a result, Bau effortlessly steps in when I am struggling to be patient or present (I do the same for him too), and I have learnt to let him.

'Mother/parenting guilt seems to be something that I have to make peace with. I remind myself and my daughter that I'm human and I will make mistakes whether I like it or not, and we both need to work on it and guide each other to make things better. So essentially, communication is the key here,' one woman I spoke to told me.

And if you are unfortunate enough to be a millennial mom, dumped into an age of mom influencers all over the internet and social media, you have it so much harder. As a *Psychology Today* article says, 'In the world of Pinterest and Instagram, it's never been harder to be a mom. Perfectionism has reached new heights.'[4]

A *Washington Post* article titled 'Millennials are tired of trying to be perfect moms', put it out there more mercilessly:

> For generations, mothers have shouldered the weight of an illusory ideal, the daunting societal standards that shape our perception of what motherhood *should* be. This pressure is particularly acute for millennial moms who arrived at parenthood in the age of social media, with a deluge of imagery and information constantly at their fingertips. There are parenting forums and TikTok stars and experts and influencers, discussing what the latest study reveals about screen time, how you should respond when your child has an emotional outburst, and why the colours you choose to decorate your child's bedroom might affect their mental health. There are friends and fellow parents, posting carefully curated snapshots of their family lives.[5]

Being a borderline millennial mom, I have had to beat this too. The constant attack by supermoms on social media about the right way to bring up children is more exhausting than the tirade that our generation had to put up with from our families and friends. I wanted to be the mother who drew smiley faces on their child's sandwich with ketchup or cut them into cute teddy shapes. These reels and videos heap perfection pressure on mothers, and double and triple their mother guilt.

'Mother's guilt used to literally kill me,' says one of my interviewees. 'I would blame myself every time the baby cried. Every illness was my fault.'

'I try to breathe through it and talk to myself and rationalize a bit,' says another mother.

'The burden of a mother's guilt is something many women grapple with, and it's rooted in the profound societal shift from the traditional archetype of what a woman should be. This shift can evoke a sense of grief and guilt because these expectations are omnipresent in our lives,' Dr Yadav says.

As a working mother, Dr Yadav herself negotiates the challenge of balancing her role as a mother and a doctor. 'And yes, I do feel guilt at times.'

To cope with this guilt, Dr Yadav has adopted a few strategies. 'Firstly, I've normalized it. I accept that as a working mother, experiencing guilt is a part of my journey. I don't resist it, suppress it, fight it or deny it. When it arises, I acknowledge it and sit with it. Secondly, I've set clear boundaries around my work to ensure I can allocate quality time to my daughter and also to my professional commitments. These boundaries help me strike a balance. Thirdly, I've examined and worked on the beliefs I hold about myself. If I believe I deserve to excel in my work and as a mother, it helps alleviate guilt. However, unrealistic beliefs such as thinking I must provide a home-cooked meal for my child every single time can contribute to guilt. So, adjusting these beliefs has been essential for me.'

Dr Yadav says that what is also important is to recognize that every mother is different. 'I recognize that I am a different kind of mother compared to my own, as times have changed. My mother was an exceptional mother who could devote all her time to me. I've come to terms with the fact that I won't be able to replicate that entirely, but I've found my own way of being a good mother while pursuing my career. When guilt arises, I use it as an opportunity to reflect on how I can do better, but most of the time, I allow myself some grace. I thoroughly enjoy my work, and by establishing clear boundaries between work and family, I've managed to navigate this journey more smoothly.'

Mothers experience a higher level of guilt when they are unable to balance home and work and this, in turn, influences their professional decisions, which may seem like choices but are actually a result of gender-based socializations and norms and hence, 'influenced choices' rather than 'free choices'. When women abandon their careers, they might say and convince themselves that it is because of their want for family time, but in reality, it is because they are unable to balance their personal and professional lives, and since society expects them to prioritize their caregiving roles anyway, it is a no-brainer that they would either leave their jobs or cut back on their hours. Women are socialized to internalize this not just through societal and familial indoctrination through their lives but also more subtly, through women's portrayal in popular media—including in advertisements—as well as through the language we use. In 2019, a research article, 'The Multiple Dimensions of Gender Stereotypes: A Current Look at Men's and Women's Characterizations of Others and Themselves', found that 'gender stereotypes often are internalized by men and women.' These stereotypes are perpetuated subtly and not so subtly in the image of the man as a dominant and adventurous personality—one who is not averse to taking risks—while women are portrayed as weak, submissive and emotional and hence, more suited to emotional and physical nurturing.[6]

It is thus unsurprising, that most of the guilt women feel in a day is related to their roles as nurturers and caregivers. And more than 96 per cent of women feel guilty at least once a day—do the math; that's feeling guilty 24/7/365.

'Women struggle mightily with the emotion of guilt. I've observed this truth for nearly thirty years as a psychotherapist, friend, mother, employer, neighbour, and in every other role I play with fellow women. When it comes to emotional well-being, guilt may be the greatest obstacle we face,' psychotherapist Nancy Colier wrote in her article titled 'The Guilt That Women Suffer'. 'What I see in my office day in and day out is this: women believe that everything that's wrong has ever been wrong and will ever go wrong is their fault. If something or someone else isn't okay, we've done something to cause it and are thereby responsible for fixing it. At the same time, women feel guilty for needing anything for themselves. The truth is women feel guilty most of the time, for most of everything. Feeling guilty is just our normal state.'

To break the cycle of guilt, we first need to be aware of how we are making everything our fault. In India, this is more direct, where everything that goes wrong in a family or outside of it, is inevitably the woman's fault. Women are raped because of their clothes, or for being somewhere with people they shouldn't have been. When women decide to become homemakers, they are lazy or want to live off their husbands, when they can't compete in the workplace, it's because they have no ambition, but then if they have ambition, they are not a team player or too aggressive to be liked or trusted. At home, when they make a decision, it's the wrong one and when they don't, they have no initiative or self-confidence.

Damned if she does, damned if she doesn't.

It is little wonder then that most Indian women go through life nervous, edgy and anxious. Such gaslighting can affect women's confidence so much that they start blaming themselves before anyone else can start. This cycle of guilt, blame and guilt is a dangerous one.

'As soon as you notice that you're turning against yourself and diving into the self-blame hole, stop and do something different—offer yourself kindness instead of criticism. Try a new path. Instead of going down into the old, stagnant, guilty rabbit hole, treat yourself differently,' Colier said in her article.[7]

Women are habitual offenders when it comes to guilt.

Women feel guilty when they accept a promotion or a job that requires them to stay out of the home for longer times, but they also feel guilty when they reject such offers prioritizing their caregiving role. We stretch ourselves thin because that feels way better than tossing and turning in bed with feelings of guilt. Guilt triggers in us at the slightest—I sometimes even feel guilty for being monosyllabic or absent-minded with my son. My partner, on the other hand, is almost always absent-minded but I have never noticed any guilt in him because of that. And while women might be habitual offenders when it comes to guilt, the most debilitating guilt comes from their relationships. We all have friends who have struggled to walk out of abusive marriages because of various guilts—sometimes, it's about the children, sometimes, it's about their families, and sometimes, merely the guilt of being the one to walk away instead of the other way around.

But advice apart, how do women actually negotiate the various guilts that seem to be a permanent part of their being?

'I do not feel guilty over of my actions today. But I used to feel guilty about ruining my husband's happy home when I walked out on him with our daughter. He hasn't forgiven me even after twenty-three years. For years, I was made to feel very selfish and guilty by my mother who was against my decision to divorce,' says

Dipsikha. 'I did feel guilty bringing up my daughter as a single mom when I was not there for her on many occasions as she was growing up due to working late or dealing with relationships etc., but I always spoke about everything with her and never sugar-coated anything. That has probably worked out well in the long run as my daughter has accepted me and my decision to lead my life as I have so far.'

Some women also feel guilty about being victims of abuse. One woman I spoke to confided in me about being sexually abused by a neighbourhood doctor when she was eight or nine. 'I have carried that guilt for over thirty-five years now. I was not able to tell my parents about the molestation because the perpetrator was a very respected person in the neighbourhood. He explained to me that whatever happened was a secret between us. I was very young and thought who would believe me over such a respected and loved man?' she says. 'I continue to live with that guilt for not speaking up and for not telling my parents as I am sure he continued to do that to other children too.'

She had put it behind her as a bad dream, but nightmares have a way of resurfacing when you least expect them to and so, she found herself married to a man who was distantly related to her abuser.

'And now I live with two guilts—not telling my parents and my partner. I often think of telling my parents but then I backtrack because what would it achieve? I also often feel like a fake person in my marriage for not having been able to confide in my partner. This makes me also question if our marriage is based on true companionship because I just can't seem to share this with my partner.'

'I don't know why I am telling you this, I don't even know you that well,' she says to me.

I knew exactly why she was telling me—women have an invisible connection to each other through shared trauma. She was telling me because although we didn't know each other at all personally, something told her I would understand. And I did. Immediately. And why won't I? I can still see clearly in my mind our neighbourhood doctor, a man in his late sixties with grandchildren my age, rubbing my non-existent eight-year-old chest after having sent my mother out to wait in the lounge to examine me. Of course, my mother didn't know any better—why can't a child be examined in front of her mother? Doctors were akin to gods in those days. I was so traumatized after two visits that I refused to go and see him after a while. I would cry and make myself ill if they mentioned going to that doctor. I was too young to know what was happening but I knew it was wrong and did not have the vocabulary to describe what he was doing to me. My parents changed the doctor, but I carry that trauma within me everywhere I go. I cannot be alone in a room with an older man ever. The guilt? When I finally spoke to my mother about it, she was silent. She didn't know what to say or how to put it right after so much time had passed. And yes, that monster under the garb of a doctor must have continued to abuse other children too, but that's not the guilt I carry. I was too young to understand what enabling means—I couldn't even get my head around what he was doing to me, how much it hurt and why it brought tears to my eyes. Talking to my mother also meant vocalizing the guilt—the subtle thought in my mind that somehow I might be responsible for the abuser's behaviour—and when you vocalize guilt, you realize it was only just vapour; the moment it's out of your mouth, its hold over you is gone.

But some guilt such as the mother's guilt or the daughter's guilt is hard to vaporize. As mothers, we are always guilty of not doing enough for our children, not being there for them enough, not keeping in touch with the changes in their lives or their studies, or their emotional state. Stay-at-home mothers feel guilty about the negative messaging they are transmitting to their children, as compared to children whose mothers work. Working mothers are forever guilty about working—not even about putting work above their children, but just the fact that they are out of the house possibly when their children go out to school or college, or when they come back. It's really a rabbit hole and believe me when I tell you, if you talk to your children, their views about you with dazzle your mind and liberate you. *Talk to your children.*

And then for women of the sandwich generation like me, middle-aged people with young children and ageing parents, it's both at the same time. As the *Psychology Today* article I referred to earlier also pointed out, one of the most poignant reasons millennial moms are emotionally exhausted is because their parents also need them as they enter their later years.

Mridvika's parents, for example, live in another country with her sibling. 'I meet them only once or twice a year. They are well into their sixties. I realize I have a finite number of years with them but not having as much access to them as my sibling makes me feel guilty that I am not doing enough for them—whether it is taking them on holidays or giving them the experiences that I wanted to give them when I was financially independent,' she says.

My parents also live in a different state and when they were able to travel, they would visit us every year. Now I only see them once or twice a year for a very short time, mostly owing to my work commitments. Both my partner and I have tried and failed to make our parents move in with us. I remember being especially guilty about my late in-laws as my husband was their only child. I would be on the phone with my mother-in-law for hours every day as if by being on the phone with her, I could prevent some misfortune from happening. And when my father-in-law's cancer went undetected for months, although he was steadily losing weight which did not raise a red flag with his physician, or when my mother-in-law broke her ankle, I felt personally responsible for these mishaps. I have stayed up many nights imagining them and my parents suffering the worst mishaps. Recently, my ailing father was in the hospital and before I could make it to Kolkata, he passed away. My first instinct was to shove the guilt and the grief away and stay busy with practical matters. I immediately paid the price for it though—I ended up in hospital a few days later with high blood pressure and a headache that even an intravenous injection of Tramadol could not heal. I know that I tried my best and dropped the ball sometimes because I just couldn't decide whether to be a mother or daughter first. I should have done many things that I realize I didn't—not deliberately, but because it is impossible for one person to function effortlessly with so much emotional load. And I failed (and will continue to fail) because between the 'should have' and the 'could have' is a human being with only a finite capacity to provide care. And yet, she does it day in and day out, and often by putting herself last. Dear women, cut yourselves some slack, You can't do it all—it was a lie to begin with; let's not perpetuate it any more. The cycle stops here with us—the now forties generation or the seventies daughters.

As caregivers, women often find themselves in a difficult position to say no.

A study on the mental health of caregivers found them to be more prone to depression and anxiety—and it is no secret that women worldwide shoulder a majority of their families' caregiving.[8] This makes me think of my mother, who despite spending all her waking hours caring for my ailing father (while she was herself in her mid-seventies) was so often made to feel like she was not doing enough by people who did not even visit my father once in months. 'I know I did my best but I still feel like a failure. Maybe I shouldn't have scolded him for not listening to me or maybe I should have not outsourced some of the care to professional caregivers,' she told me after my father passed. I spent a lot of time trying to deconstruct this guilt because I felt it was important that she spent the rest of her years without being burdened with the caregiver guilt on top of all the other guilt she has had to struggle with throughout her life. This guilt of outsourcing caregiving to professional caregivers is one that is particularly close to women in India because we are still made to feel inadequate, or not loving or caring enough if we pay money to someone to help us with it. This is why we have no quality institutions that can take care of elderly, ailing parents (especially from certain degenerative diseases like Alzheimer's or Parkinson's or dementia) or living communities for the elderly, even though it's been a reality for years in our country that the young often migrate out of the state or the country in search of greener pastures.

I have walked this walk of guilt with my mother at every point in time while I have known that she should not be the primary caregiver at her age—I should be. And acting on that, I brought them over to live with me right around the time the deadly second run of the Covid-19 pandemic was unleashed on us. We all tested positive and dealt with it okay. But a close relative called to taunt me: 'They were fine here all this time and did not get infected during the first wave—you take them and they are sick right away?' I had actually asked them to come to stay with me because my mother could not manage to get herself and my father vaccinated, owing to his mobility issues, despite people claiming that 'they were keeping them safe'. The moment they were here, I got them vaccinated and all of us probably picked up the infection from the hospital. The second wave of the Covid-19 pandemic was brutal—I don't think it spared anyone. While most of us accepted that we got the infection and isolated ourselves, many more just went about their business claiming it was just a 'fever'. But you see when women are being guilt-tripped, they will not think of all that they have done right but only focus on what has gone wrong. Women hear that they are wrong all the time—maybe the circumstances are different, the characters, too, but guilt-tripping women is everyone's, especially men's, favourite pastime in this country. These guilt trips for me often came from people who would only show up in emergencies, but otherwise would just leave my mother alone to shoulder my father's caregiving responsibilities.

Damned if she does, damned if she doesn't.

While I did not play a role in his infection, I did everything humanly possible to make sure he recovered well. I don't let others guilt trip me because people have never really mattered to me that much. Early in life, I realized that people, apart from your immediate family, were there to pull you down, mock you, criticize you when your back was turned, and wish that you would fail—especially if you were a woman who had tasted some amount of success in your personal or professional life. But what I suffer from greatly is self-guilt—the guilt that I lob at myself.

That day when my father's oxygen levels were dropping and we were failing in getting a hospital bed for him, I picked him up (literally—as he could barely walk by that time) and rushed him to the hospital. I was Covid-19 positive too, and I could barely stand because my infection was the worst among all of us, owing to my asthma and sleep apnoea. 'I'd tested positive but no one was coming to help my father. No one from the authorities has called to check on us, nor has any health worker visited. I was desperate and so I decided to head out, in my Covid-positive state, to get him the care he needed,' I had written in an article for the *Business Insider*. I took him to a hospital that was catering only to Covid-19 patients.[9] After the attendants wheeled him away for the scan, I just sank into a nearby chair, my whole body shaking from the exertion. That was the first time I had ventured out of my room where I had been near-unconscious for two days. But the attendant was soon at my side: 'We need you to come and help us—your father is not cooperating with us for the scan.' So, I scampered to the radiology room and my father was still in his wheelchair—when he saw me, his face broke into a smile that broke my heart right then and there. When I helped him get onto the examination bed, he was calm and cooperative, and the scan went smoothly. And from that day onwards, I have been living with the guilt that if it was me who was providing him the caregiving, would he have been happier? How fair was it to dump his caregiving on my seventy-year-old mother? But there are only reasonable answers to these questions—I live away in Delhi, I have a high-pressured job for which I travel a lot, along with a growing son and two dogs, and my parents wouldn't move in with me to make things a little bit easier. And why would they? After all, they had a set life and their own home in Kolkata; both of them earned a pension and had always been fiercely independent. What we come back to again and again is that because women provide a majority of the caregiving, no one has really thought of creating institutions to make it easier for them. We expect women to study and work, but we also expect them to do all that without shirking their caregiving duties. And then we blame them for dropping out of education and employment. An IMF working paper in 2020 found that Japan's voluntary six-week economic shutdown in response to the Covid-19 pandemic primarily carried out in April, had disproportionately affected women, owing to the 'guilt gap'. This gap is rooted in societal pressures that lead women to shoulder more professional sacrifices. The repercussions have been evident as close to a million women, particularly those in temporary or part-time roles, left the workforce between December and April.[10]

Caregiving is a mess in this country and women are suffering for it.

Roberta Satow, in her book, *Doing the Right Thing: Taking Care of Your Elderly Parents Even if They Didn't Take Care of You*, says that the caregiving guilt is complex and sometimes has to do with 'not meeting other people's expectations' or 'not meeting our own'.[11]

'There is the guilt we feel when we don't do things that we think we should. These "shoulds" are injunctions that we have not completely internalized as our own. When you say, "I should visit my mother every day," it really means you imagine someone else thinks you should. Perhaps, you imagine your relatives think you should visit your mother every day. When you think, "I should make dinner for my family instead of visiting my mother after work," you are not saying you think that's right or that's what you wish to do. Rather, you are expressing the feeling that other people, perhaps your husband, think that it is the right thing to do. Conflicting "shoulds" can be quite anxiety-provoking, making you feel torn in many directions,' Satow writes.

So what do we do then? Stop and think about these 'shoulds'? But even if we do identify them, is it so easy to ignore them, especially in a society like India where women are expected to shoulder a majority of the care burden—looking after young children, elderly parents as well as their in-laws? I would see my mother-in-law running around between her mother-in-law and other elderly relatives who lived alone in the neighbourhood. At the time, she herself was in her late sixties and yet, she felt compelled to take care of their needs even when she was unwell—if she couldn't a day, she would feel extremely guilty for missing out on checking on them. Nobody told her to do this; she didn't need to do this and yet, she did—not just because she thought of expectations but also out of sheer empathy and the fact that there is such a huge caregiving gap in our country.

Elderly care, especially, is completely non-existent. Estimates suggest that the elderly population in India will reach 324 million by the year 2050. And yet, there are only a handful of services dedicated to elderly care in India, and most of them are expensive and not always very efficient. The public health system has next to no focus on elderly care and it is completely dependent on the invisible labour of women.

There are many 'shoulds' in my mind too, some of them completely random, but they are there. There are days when separating the 'should' from what I 'can' is difficult, but accepting these days is the first step to overcoming this guilt. Instead of telling myself what I should have done, I found ways to help relieve my mother's caregiving burden sometimes by researching and sending her patient aids so that some of the care was automated. Of late, I have realized that what she really needs is to talk to me every day—so I call her every day, no matter what happens, where I am placed or how I am placed, even if it's for a few seconds.

'As an only child, I suffered a great deal of daughter's guilt. I tried my best but still felt like I was not doing enough. But once I learnt to deal with my mother's guilt, I learnt to deal with all other kinds of guilt, too.' says Natasha. 'There are still instances where I feel that I am falling short of her expectations of me, but I don't let that feeling take me prisoner any longer.'

I am reminded of my friend's golden advice—*watch yourself closely at all times*. Yes, it's exhausting, but that's the way we bring change in our lives and break out of the shackles that society has put on us—both the visible and invisible ones.

Look after yourself—if not you, then who? Talk to someone about what you are going through and the feelings you are feeling. Emotions need an outlet and if that is not a person for you, it could be a journal or something else—like talking to plants. Did you know that in the United States, 48 per cent of the people surveyed talk to their plants?[12] 62 per cent of them said that talking to plants improved their mental health. A 2015 study in the *Journal of Physiological Anthropology* found that 'active interaction with indoor plants can reduce physiological and psychological stress.'[13] When people talk to plants or spend time around them, it lowers the body's stress response by calming the sympathetic nervous system, which is responsible for the 'fight or flight' response, leading to a sense of relaxation. Interacting with houseplants also lowers our blood pressure. Every morning, I spend 10–15 minutes watering my plants, admiring them and spraying the leaves. This routine really sets me up for the day as it creates a sense of well-being and calmness. What else it does do? It helps me work through emotions—much like when I walk or jog in the mornings. I find any solitary activity to be very useful in addressing feelings of guilt, resentment, anger or just anxiety and sadness. Doing things alone is a much-ignored form of self-care. When we are with others, our caregiving traits take over along with feelings of guilt or anxiety. When I am in company, I often feel anxious just thinking if everyone is having a good time, if they are okay, maybe we should have gone somewhere else or ordered something else—there is no time either to process present or past emotions. It is only when we are alone that we can completely relax, focus on our feelings and work through them.

Women often struggle with guilt when prioritizing themselves. I wish there was a practical handbook for managing this guilt. I deal with it by recognizing my limits and reminding myself that I can't do everything.

What I have found helpful also is talking about my guilt to my family and they have been quick to assuage my fears. And after those conversations, I felt almost silly for not articulating my guilt before to my family or even my friends. The crux of dealing with guilt is to understand that you are not in it alone. No one will say anything or stop you if you want to do it all because they are so used to that being the norm, but when you talk about the guilt that propels you to do it all and be perfect, they will understand, and maybe even course-correct. But often, women are unable to talk freely for fear of being judged and find themselves forever playing into the trope of the uncomplaining, resilient superwoman, who can do it all without a word of protest.

And when you can't talk about what really bothers you, you are in a constant mental loop of justifying its existence and your choices, much like a hamster running on his wheel. This is exactly why the most important intervention at this point in time would be to create safe and empathetic spaces for women, where they can understand the gender stereotypes that make them prisoners in this game of expectations, start talking about their feelings and brainstorm ways to address them.

Have we truly provided women with safe spaces where they can openly talk and share? What often exists is a sort of forced sisterhood, where women often feel pressured to maintain an image that doesn't match the reality of their daily lives. Moreover, when grouped into economic empowerment initiatives, women's unique sociocultural backgrounds are frequently overlooked, leading them to feel inadequate or underachieving. The communities we build for women often mirror male-oriented social structures, sometimes merely serving as a box-checking exercise. As a result, women continue to suppress their true selves and desires.

To create safe spaces for women, first and foremost, we have to work at ending the trust deficit between women. We have to make them unlearn the patriarchal socialization that has pitted them against each other for the approval of male figures. Start talking to your families first—in fact, if you have children, start talking to them first. Children are wise beyond their years and the umbilical cord really does a good job—they are indescribably connected to us. Once you start talking, you won't be able to stop. Talking about the guilt is the only way to tame it.

The daughter's guilt can be especially vicious in our society—after a woman is married in India, somehow, the expectation is that she will take on all the burdens of her marital home while relinquishing those of her parents. But women have always taken care of their elderly parents—sometimes in secret, sometimes by openly rebelling and sometimes by balancing their other care responsibilities. Here, the 'care of the marital family must always be prioritized' is the unwritten rule that women feel compelled to follow. These unwritten rules and unreasonable expectations of women create a maze of guilt in their minds. But if you take out the expectations and only focus on the emotions, you will be okay. You will know what to do. Concrete action will kill the devil in your mind. It will also set a precedent. Precedents are important to decimating socialization and socialization-based expectations.

So, start by refusing to be overwhelmed by guilt. Make a realistic list of your caregiving responsibilities and prioritize them based on your emotional capacity rather than societal expectations. Yes, this approach might meet resistance, both from your own ingrained beliefs and from others, but remember, *no meaningful change has ever occurred without some pushback.*

This concept of wrestling with guilt isn't limited to just the daily responsibilities.

I have friends who still feel guilty about the death of a parent although they had nothing to do with it. They were the best daughters and best caregivers and yet, they blame themselves for reaching a little late or getting caught up with something, and they connect it with their parent's death. It's a rabbit hole that one should not go down into. When your emotions are overtaking your reason, sit yourself down and make that 'should' list. *Be kind to yourself.*

'There are days when I am a super boss and I fall short of being a good spouse. But I have accepted that,' says Mridvika. 'The moment I accepted that I started feeling less angry. I started feeling less frustrated and I think, I started feeling a lot more content than what I was able to achieve.'

We need to also remember that while women don't often inherit their ancestral property, what they do inherit is the trauma of women who have come before them—great-grandmothers, grandmothers, mothers or any other female relative. The path to salvation runs through the by-lanes of this inherited trauma, and identifying, understanding and addressing this trauma is of paramount importance.

6

The Inheritance of Trauma: Understanding Our Pain

> 'Maybe the pain is like me, desperate to be seen in the lives of those around me.'
>
> —Sondra Charbadze

A few years ago, during a conversation with my mother, I came to know that my maternal grandmother had committed suicide when she was merely in her thirties and a young widow with three children. No one knows for sure what happened, why she took the step she did and orphaned her three young children. Did her trauma pass down to me? I survived a suicide attempt—the incident is still shrouded in mystery for me. Yes, I was emotionally disturbed, and yes, I was coping badly, but I was in therapy and my therapist never thought I was a suicide risk. The day when I downed one month's worth of sleeping pills, it was like someone else's emotions had attached to mine—suddenly making it all exhaustingly unbearable.

Women inherit trauma.

Women deal with so much trauma—not just the trauma of their lives but also intergenerational trauma, which is the process of passing the impact of traumatic experiences to successive generations, affecting women and their families. It can result from various roots such as domestic and sexual abuse, alcohol and drug addiction, and historical conflicts like war or famine. The symptoms of intergenerational trauma can be similar to complex PTSD and may include denial, depersonalization, isolation, memory loss, nightmares and substance abuse, among others.

Breaking the cycle of intergenerational trauma requires open discussions about trauma experiences, sharing wisdom and raising awareness about the issue; talking to children about inherited trauma and its origins is essential. Seeking therapeutic treatment from specialized psychiatrists and counsellors is also crucial in helping women cope with their symptoms and heal from trauma. By understanding the causes and effects of intergenerational trauma and seeking professional support, women can work towards breaking the cycle and empowering themselves and future generations.

'Traumatic experiences can take many forms,' says an article on understanding intergenerational trauma and its effects on the Healthline website. 'You might, for instance, find yourself facing long-term emotional distress after discovering a partner's infidelity, losing your sibling in a car accident, or coping with the sudden illness and death of a beloved pet. Yet, certain types of trauma can have a far more profound impact. Major, large-scale traumatic events often don't affect only those who survive them. The toll of these experiences can reverberate across generations.'[1]

How does trauma manifest in our lives? Trauma therapist Canh Tran says that trauma might have simple manifestations in our lives, such as always feeling sleepy and lethargic, having trouble falling asleep, taking recourse to substance abuse to cope, more intense anger or irritability and a sense of complete detachment. It can also affect personal relationships and bring feelings of isolation and alienation along with physical manifestations such as headaches, migraine, stomach aches, spiked body temperature and shakiness. In the article, Tran said that intergenerational trauma requires a more empathetic response. 'It's moving from, "What's wrong with you?" to "What happened to you?" to "How have you learned to survive?" and eventually, "What can we do to support your healing moving forward?"'

For the longest time ever, I didn't understand that what I was experiencing was intergenerational trauma. And in India, the Partition and personal and private experiences of violence have all contributed to who we have become. My maternal grandmother's suicide was a cross my mother bore for most of her life—she had no answers and no one to ask the questions that haunted her. Ultimately, she ended up stuck in an abusive marriage. If I think back, I do see how difficult it was for her to connect to people or even her family. There was always an aloofness in her, which I believe provoked my father's masculinity. He interpreted it as disobedience or plain disdain. As a child, I was pained by my mother's aloofness, her inability to smile or just be. When I began to look at her life through the lens of trauma, everything fell into place. Where it starts getting complicated is that I am not the recipient of just my grandmother's and mother's trauma. I am the recipient of more trauma than a human should possibly deal with. My paternal grandparents had to flee Bangladesh owing to violence—overnight, they had to leave behind their families, homes, livelihood and life to begin anew in India. There is no cause to think that trauma was not passed down to me.

For years I wondered why therapy didn't work for me completely and then I realized—it was because we were treating the wounds that were visible, not the ones I had inherited. What helped me the most was learning about my family's history, asking uncomfortable questions, and thinking and writing about them—the more I talked and wrote, the more I could feel the knots in my mind opening up one by one. I am still working through all of my inherited trauma and I have found a way to cope with them, but it's a long journey.

You can't rewrite the history of your life—you cannot go back in time and undo the trauma that was passed down to you. But you can start by asking questions and trying to get to the root of the trauma you are carrying in your body.

'Women, since the beginning of recorded history, have been traumatized through physical, sexual, emotional and economic abuse. This has happened on such a large scale that when we are writing our histories, we don't even recognize it as trauma. All major cultures operate under a patriarchal system with women being treated as second-class citizens, a status that has allowed men to rape, beat, murder, mutilate, starve and control women for thousands of years. There is no debate that these things have occurred—it is a matter of record. And now that we are starting to understand more about the ways that trauma impacts not only an individual but the entire community and its subsequent generations, we should be looking at the trauma of women differently,' Claire Ryder, a US-based clinical psychologist wrote in an article, 'Women: What We Pass Down', in 2019.[2]

A 2023 study on intergenerational trauma in the context of the 1947 India–Pakistan Partition found that intergenerational trauma 'can present itself in a wide-ranging variety of symptoms, including hypervigilance, mistrust, high anxiety, insomnia, low self-esteem, nightmares, aloofness and panic attacks, among many others.' It might also 'have a negative impact on the immune system, causing it to be either hyperactive or not active enough. This, in turn, is associated with a greater likelihood of developing autoimmune diseases . . . It can also manifest itself in the form of unresolved thoughts and emotions about a traumatic event, poor parent–child relationships, a sense of emotional detachment, and a possibility of developing personality disorders, negative patterns of behaviour or even negligible to no acknowledgement of possible mental illnesses.'[3]

It can also present itself as anger. When one of her clients came to her after therapy failed to address her anger issues, Bardoloi tried the controversial family constellation therapy to reach the roots of her anger. 'She has had so much anger,' Bardoloi says. 'She has had four failed relationships owing to this anger and yet, there was no immediate reason for her anger. Every time she went on a date, all she felt was anger at the person she was meeting. She wanted to be in an intimate relationship but her anger was coming in the way.'

As their sessions progressed, Bardoloi could see that the girl was carrying her grandmother's trauma. 'She was well-educated and had a loving childhood. Strangely, she had a lot of anger against men although no man had hurt her yet. And then we found out that her grandmother was raped—a trauma so severe that it could not be processed or mourned in one generation . . . Breaking generational curses is possible through self-enlightenment and recognizing our connection to our ancestors. It's okay to walk alone and pursue personal growth while acknowledging and processing emotions without letting them hinder our progress,' says Bardoloi. 'What's not processed in one generation has to be processed in the next.'

Too many women experience intergenerational trauma from abuse even though they might not have faced it themselves. Such trauma affects their sense of safety, their personal or romantic relationships, and consequently, their self-worth.

Bad parenting too can leave trauma in children and often stems from the trauma the parents have inherited. 'In India, a lot of bad parenting is justified as cultural. We do things to children we wouldn't do to our worst enemy, probably because we fear retaliation from our enemy. My mother thought that if I were the perfect child, then I could be saved from the hurt she experienced when she was a child. My father thought being funny would make him more accepted among his peers. I was in my mid-thirties when I realized that what I had experienced as a child was abuse. But what do you expect when most Indians beat and emotionally manipulate their children and think it is good parenting?' Subuhi Safvi, a trauma coach based in Delhi, says. 'As a nation, we have inherited so much trauma. Our grandparents went through the partition, our parents have experienced riots and wars, and we are still caught in the middle of those two worlds. Women are diminished all the time—they are told they're incomplete without husbands, that their worth is only in being caregivers and nurturers, and that they must always prioritize everyone else. On top of that, we have few women in positions of power to speak to about our struggles. And, let's be honest, most, if not all of us have experienced at least some form of sexual harassment in our lives. This is trauma that would hold anyone back. And it holds us back, too.'

In 2014, a first-of-its-kind study titled 'Unresolved trauma in mothers: intergenerational effects and the role of reorganization' that examined how secure children feel in their relationships, especially when it comes to how trauma and attachment patterns are passed down between generations, found that mothers with unresolved trauma affect the attachment they can form with their children 'potentially contributing to the intergenerational transmission of trauma'.[4]

When I read about intergenerational trauma, so much of my own trauma made sense and my mother's detachment made sense. Growing up, I always felt that my mother was emotionally unavailable while my father was always emotionally available but also abusive towards my mother. These contradictions created such a maze in my mind that I kept running circles around it. And then it all made sense when I learnt about my maternal grandmother's suicide, and connected the dots with my mother's unresolved trauma over the abandonment she must have felt when her mother chose to orphan her and her siblings and die by suicide. There must have been so many questions in her mind that, over time, just solidified into a mass of grief—a stony wall with not a single window. Since she couldn't speak up, couldn't challenge the system or try and change it, she let the trauma pile up within her instead.

Understanding my mother's detachment through the lens of intergenerational trauma made me realize something crucial about our society. It's not just individual families that carry these silent burdens; our entire societal structure often mirrors this pattern of unspoken pain and suppressed voices.

Our society functions on women's invisible and non-valued labour. It also functions on their silence. We Indians often take pride in our family system, but this system is actually standing on a structure that is hollow from the inside. The structure, in turn, is still standing because women have chosen to not speak out or voice their opinions and concerns as much as they should. More often than not, they quietly accept their roles and the conditions they must face without any protest or demand for change. A major reason behind this is that we have been taught to suffer in silence—in fact, it is made out to be a virtue of some sort.

Patriarchy has not just alienated women from each other but also pitted them against each other. But we are beginning to start questioning this hypocritical, soulless system. This is a potent, if silent, movement that will only grow stronger with time. As more and more women join this movement, there will be more and more space for them to be honest with each other. They will stop swallowing the truth and start calling out the injustices they made peace with, they will stop pretending to be happy and instead, look for true happiness—the definition of which would be theirs and only theirs. There is strength in numbers, and our numbers are growing every day.

'There is a systemic demonization of women and negation of them being a power structure. Then there is discrimination against single women, especially widows and divorcees. We have been divided so spectacularly through various generations that we have become fragmented,' says Bardoloi. 'Men have fought wars and hunted together—their brotherhood is very strong and it is celebrated, while sisterhood is laughed at or ridiculed. When women get together to talk to each other, it's dismissed as "gossiping". This systematic oppression and negation of our power as individuals and a community.'

For a long time, Bardoloi too grappled with this trauma that led her to people-please and over-give. She felt like she was not good enough and couldn't love herself. 'I over-gave so that I would be appreciated,' she says. 'But over-giving is not sacrifice, it is a psychological issue.' But while trying to heal her clients, Bardoloi has been able to heal herself too.

'I have learnt that there is nothing more valuable than self-love.'

However, she says healing is a process and 'we are the first generation that is trying to call out the toxicity in our lives.'

So, yes, be kind to yourselves.

Like with everything else in women's lives, trauma too often remains shrouded in silence, and if that trauma has some taboo attached to it, then the silence reverberates through generations.

Women are discouraged from talking about grief or showing grief openly. When we talk about grief in India, we always equate overcoming it with strength. The point of grief is to overcome it. Is that really so? Shouldn't the point of grief really be to feel it, face it and get help when it begins to affect your normal functioning? But how do you get help for grief when it's not even considered a mental illness in this country?

What is this obsession with standing up straight after every misfortune, picking up the pieces and moving along? It is almost as if we are afraid of grief—of witnessing it and having to deal with it. As if just by association, it will weaken or disable us.

Recently, a friend suddenly lost her husband. He was only in his mid-forties. On her Facebook post, there was comment after comment asking her to be strong and to move on. It's almost like her friends wanted her to move on because they didn't have the time to wait around for her to heal. I messaged her privately, telling her that she must wallow in her grief—being strong was overrated. I was not sure what her response would be.

'I haven't been able to break down as yet. The pressure to be strong at all times is stifling. Wallowing in my grief is a luxury,' she wrote back.

I am sure my friend too tried her best to stay strong—at least for the sake of her daughter. To not show her grief—to try and stand up straight when she would probably want nothing more than to curl up in bed. This may be the trauma she will pass on to her daughter.

Let children see their mothers in all their emotions—that's how they will learn to process their own grief. When we clamp down our emotions, they are going nowhere but getting passed down to the next generations. We are setting a trauma pattern. In a country like India, where women cannot be themselves even in their deaths, there is no other release for trauma but to be passed down through generations of women as unprocessed grief, anger or even resentment. Here, women's suicides are routinely dressed up as natural deaths, dowry deaths are masked as accidents, and sexual assaults are a shame for the family and the survivor. Women are not allowed to feel, grieve or be who they are.

And then there is the trauma of caste and gender identities. Women are not a homogenous group—they come with different histories, different scars and different struggles. To try and write a book that would work for every woman in India is not just audacious, but also impractical and perhaps, delusional too. But what I intend to do is collect and document women's lived experiences and their coping strategies, and lay them out in one place—a community, a safe and non-judgmental space, where you come to learn but also to unlearn. While there are no substitutions to institutional support and normative behaviour change, we could start by talking about our experiences with each other, with our families, and with society at large. For Indian women, intergenerational trauma is debilitating. For Dalit women, it is structural—it is what they live with and struggle with, day in and day out. It is a trauma that leaves behind deep emotional and mental scars. The structural dehumanization, violence and subjugation on three levels—gender, caste and class—are beyond the understanding of a non-Dalit and that includes me too. However, the violence and oppression have continued to the present day and hence, it is a trauma that continues to be handed down through generations.

Transgenerational trauma involves the transmission of emotional wounds and pain from one generation to another. My grandmother's suicide cast a shadow over my mother and consequently, on me. In a society that has historically stigmatized mental health issues and struggles, such occurrences were often swept under the rug. The first step towards healing is acknowledging the past. Sharing stories can be a powerful way to reclaim the narrative and find solidarity. I have the opportunity to break the silence surrounding my grandmother's tragedy and initiate open conversations about mental health. While discussing my grandmother's suicide is challenging, I am still doing it. The most difficult part of this journey was to keep talking to my mother about this. In the beginning, she was hesitant and uncomfortable. But when I persisted, she started talking more freely. In our conversations, I could feel we had created a safe space and many knots in our minds were being opened. For me talking about my grandmother, whom I never met, is a way to honour her, the tragedy that her life was and the suffering that led her to kill herself.

So, when I wrote my first book, it was uncomfortable but I spoke to my mother about my grandmother. In the beginning, the conversations would be halting and I would search for ways to ask questions that could be triggers while my mother, on her part, would struggle with how much to tell. But over a few of those, both of us understood we were undoing important knots and spoke freely. I do believe that our relationship took a new turn following those conversations—my mother has always been angsty, something she has passed on to me, but today, I can understand that angst better. I deal with it better and I am more patient. It was the same when we started talking about my parents' abusive marriage—it took time for me to ask the right questions and for her to find the courage to answer truthfully, but we got there eventually and we are better for it.

Mother–daughter conversations are so important to heal generational trauma. These conversations must be around educating ourselves about us—who are we? Where do we come from? What tragedy, what pain, what struggles define us? India's mental health landscape is evolving, with more resources available for women to access therapy and support groups. Empowerment comes through knowledge and understanding, enabling you to recognize patterns of behaviour or thought that might be rooted in generational trauma.

Women in India often grapple with societal norms that can exacerbate the impact of intergenerational trauma. The pressure to conform to traditional roles and expectations can hinder the healing process. It's important to recognize that healing is not synonymous with forgetting one's culture. Rather, it involves adapting cultural values to promote mental well-being. Integrating practices like meditation and yoga or engaging with community support systems, can bridge the gap between cultural heritage and modern coping mechanisms.

Forming strong support networks is crucial for women dealing with transgenerational trauma. Seek out friends, family members, or support groups that provide a safe space for sharing emotions and experiences. Creating a circle of understanding individuals can provide validation, empathy, and a sense of belonging. Additionally, seeking professional therapy can offer targeted guidance in navigating the complexities of trauma.

Discovering that my maternal grandmother died by suicide brought about a whirlwind of emotions and questions, but it also brought me the answers I have been seeking throughout my life. I can say with certainty today that the trauma I carry in my body is not mine alone, it is the trauma of my maternal grandmother, who died by suicide, the trauma of my paternal grandmother, who had to escape her home and life in the dead of the night for another country, and definitely the trauma of my mother, trapped in an abusive marriage. I am not one—I am all of them as well.

Millions of girls in India have been born knowing that they have been exceptionally lucky because millions of others were killed in the womb. The trauma of female foeticide is complex and deep-rooted, and encompasses the cultural, social and psychological dimensions that stem from the son preference prevalent in Indian families. The practice of aborting female foetuses, as a result, has contributed to skewed sex ratios and negative consequences for women's status and mental well-being in this country as women who experience the trauma of foeticide and gender-based discrimination may internalize feelings of guilt, shame and unworthiness.

In our country, a vast majority of women grow up feeling like they're not wanted or loved, which makes them doubt their own value. What this feeling creates is the burden of thankfulness—women who escaped the trauma of being unwanted feel gratitude so deeply that they tend to overlook or accept many of the unfair demands and rules that a male-dominated society puts on them. We are always thankful for what we have because the alternative could be so much worse.

I wonder if this is also not an intergenerational trauma that women carry in their bodies—the feeling of being unwanted or coming from a line of women many of whom might have been unwanted, surely must affect our worldview and how we view ourselves.

'My parents never treated me any differently because I was a girl but my grandmother did. I was so grateful to my parents for always having my back and never making me feel like I was a burden to them or even unwanted, that I wanted to be perfect in everything I did. If I was not perfect, especially at my marital home, I would be failing them. And every time I did fail at something, shame would wash over me—I would feel so powerless,' my friend, Ishita,* once told me. And I knew exactly where she was coming from because that is how I had felt most of my life too. In India, parents do, however, play the shame card, especially with daughters. 'Whatever you do will come back to us. It will bring shame on our upbringing, remember that' is a spoken-sometimes-unspoken sentiment that

---

* Name changed.

haunts us throughout our lives. 'It is important that we talk about it instead of pushing it under the carpet. It's important that we call out our parents and take a look at how embedded this is in us. I talk to my daughter a lot and she can pull me up any time if I unconsciously try to put the burden of shame or the onus of perfection on her. And this is how we will be able to end this cycle of shame and unreal expectations of women.'

As we delve into these deep-rooted issues of shame and perfection that burden many women from a young age, it's crucial to also recognize another significant aspect that is often overlooked: the trauma associated with women's work experiences.

I remember very early on, I wanted to emulate my mother and become a cop—it was my single ambition. But every time I would broach the topic, my mother would get furious. 'No—absolutely not,' she would say. 'Take a pick of any other profession but not the police force.' I didn't understand where she was coming from then, but today, when I have worked as a journalist for over twenty-two years, I know if I had a daughter, I would tell her to be whatever she wants but not a journalist. The struggle of women in the workplace has a detrimental effect on women's empowerment. It is such a struggle to stay working in male-dominated careers—there is so much systemic push to get women out or to not let them grow, that it is traumatic. It is why women get sucked into so-called 'feminine jobs'.

Psychologist Maya Borgueta wrote in her article, 'When it's not just burnout: Recognizing trauma in the workplace', that some of her clients' relationships 'with their bosses sound a lot like the type of emotional abuse people can experience in relationships with an abusive partner or parent.' This, she says, might come across in the form of verbal abuse, harsh criticism or gaslighting.[5] As a woman in male-dominated newsrooms, I have faced all of the above in addition to the bullying that is reserved specifically for women. In most of the places I worked, they would gang up on me because I refused to attend get-togethers and gatherings. 'She is too arrogant' was the buzz. Maybe I was, but that did not affect my work—I was as brilliant a journalist then as I am now. I have never let anything compromise the quality of my work and yet, I had to routinely fight for the stories I wanted to do, for my stories not to be killed. And yes, I handled them the way they needed to be handled—by ignoring them—but they left a trail of scars in my mind. Earlier this year, when I accepted an editorial consultancy job and stopped reporting for news publications, it was not because I was done telling stories (I still have so many stories to tell), but because I was done having to prove myself over and over again in a space created by and for men, and where throughout my career, I have only been treated as an interloper. If women begin to connect work with trauma, I don't think it will be easy to bring them back to the workforce or retain them. What has helped me deal with work trauma is the understanding that quitting is not an option until you have fought your hardest. I have fought hard throughout my life in work spaces, against being pushed out, and unfortunately, I have only ever lost those battles. But the war is still raging in me—though, its expressions are different now, better focused, perhaps. By not emulating male leader behaviour but crafting my own style of leadership that is based on fairness and equality. We must try not to let trauma define us. Instead, we need to let it empower us.

The story of the Indian woman is not a single narrative—it is a coming together of many experiences and stories of double marginalization owing to caste, class, race and gender or sexual identities. Noted feminist, the late Kamla Bhasin, once said in a keynote speech, 'What Is Feminism?':[6]

> When we look at the world through women's eyes, we are looking at the world through the eyes of the most exploited, most oppressed, because amongst the poor women are the poorest, amongst the Dalits women are the most Dalit, amongst the Blacks women are the most oppressed. When we see the world through the eyes of women, only then do we get a perspective of the marginalized, the excluded, and the oppressed.

When we speak of women's experiences, we are acknowledging a reality where intersectionality is not just a concept but a lived truth. Women find themselves at the crossroads of multiple forms of discrimination and marginalization. Among the poor, they often bear the brunt of poverty's harshest consequences; among Dalits, they endure not only the weight of caste-based discrimination but also gender-based discrimination, making them the most vulnerable within an already oppressed community and among Black communities, they often face intersecting racial and gender biases that compound their struggles.

Women are not a homogenous group, and neither are their struggles nor their coping mechanisms—for we fight with what we have access to, the history we come from and the trauma we carry in our bodies.

Abha,* who works in the development sector, was raised by a single mother, who worked as a sanitation worker in the local municipality. Her father died early. For many years, she did not realize that she was carrying the trauma her father faced as a Dalit in India.

'My father always wanted to study and be someone, but given that he was born a Dalit, he could never fulfil this dream. He became frustrated and quite sadistic. He suffered from many ailments which meant he didn't work,' she remembers. 'He was born in trauma and he passed it onto his children—us.'

She first came across this concept of transgenerational trauma when she was studying for her undergraduate degree. 'I had a module on psychiatry, mental health and counselling. After studying that, I realized everyone in my family was struggling with some kind of mental health issues. We all needed counselling.'

But Abha is also carrying the trauma of her mother's story. While her mother had a better life than her father, her parents witnessed India's struggle for independence.

---

* Name changed.

Her great-grandfather had moved the family to the city as he felt they were being marginalized in their village. 'My mother's first five siblings died because of various diseases. They also struggled through a period of drought. My mother always had the responsibility to look after her six younger siblings. She could not study more than class seven. She was pulled into household work and caregiving from a very young age. I have always noted the sadness in my mother's eyes that she was not deemed important enough for her father—they were a comparatively wealthy family—to make a more informed decision about her marriage.'

Abha's father was addicted to alcohol, poor and did not have a proper home. But he belonged to the same caste, and that became the most important consideration. 'She was constantly told that if she did not get married within her caste, she wouldn't be respected. And she tries to do that to me too, although very subtly. During our conversations, she would slip in how she educated me so much so I would understand the importance of marrying within our caste. It's her trauma talking.'

'I have felt my mother's trauma—of being the sixth child, the one who was the least important of her siblings and yet, the most responsible one, and most importantly, of coping with an alcoholic spouse and poverty,' Abha says.

This trauma has defined Abha's relationship with her mother. Sometimes they are good with each other, sometimes they are in conflict.

'The more I read, the more I become aware of the intergenerational drama that exists between both of us,' she says.

'I would always get frustrated with her and think "Why is she saying this? Why is she doing this? Why can't she be normal like other mothers?" but the day I learnt to put her behaviour in the context of her trauma, I could understand her better.'

'The trauma that people from marginalized communities face is completely unique. Our trauma defines the way we talk and how we behave. For example, when a wealthy, upper-caste family sends their daughter out of town to study, they book a nice hostel for them and are concerned about the view outside their daughter's window or if they serve fruits in the canteen. But as a first-generation learner, my mother would ask me questions like did I even find a place to live? Upper-caste people live with concerns, we live with trauma that comes from a place of social and economic insecurity,' she continued.

In 2018, Christina Dhanaraj, a Dalit artist, wrote in an article: 'I'm a Dalit woman and my mental health matters. What we need is an overhaul.' She went on to say that 'external circumstances defined by caste atrocities, untouchability, oppression, lack of resources, and prevalence of microaggressions, over a prolonged period of time, could have resulted in intergenerational trauma for Dalit communities, which now is being further compounded by present-day caste violence and discrimination.'[7]

'When I was in school, my classmates would not eat with me. Back then, something like this was quite normalized. Nobody cared. There was one more girl who was from the Dalit community, and we stuck together. Our classmates called us *chor chamar*,'* Malvika, an artist and a Dalit rights activist from Bihar says.

From her company's HR asking her about her caste to a former lover's mother raining abuse on her and her father for being a Dalit, or another insisting on her visiting Hindu temples with him despite her repeated assertions that she was a Buddhist, Malvika has been negotiating her trauma one day at a time.

'When my last relationship ended, I turned a corner,' she says. She had caught her then-partner trying to reason with his mother on the phone to agree to his marriage with Malvika. 'She was saying the filthiest things about me and my father. Calling us that same name that I have heard so many times in my life—chor chamar. And my partner was quietly listening to her tirade—not standing up for me, the person he was supposedly in love with and wanted to marry. This means somewhere deep down, he, too, believed what she was saying about us and our caste. I walked out of his house that day and never looked back. I haven't spoken to him since.'

---

* *Chor Chamar* is a derogatory term in India, combining *chor* (thief) and *chamar* (a caste-associated term). Its use not only perpetuates harmful caste-based stereotypes and discrimination, but also unfairly labels a specific community as thieves, reinforcing negative and unfounded biases.

Following this traumatizing incident, Malvika returned to Bihar and took up Madhubani painting—a traditional heritage art form in the state.

She visited various villages to learn the art form. 'Madhubani paintings reflect a lot of stories from Hindu mythology—Ramayana, Mahabharat, Krishna Leela. I also painted all of those because I had to learn them but somehow, I could not connect with them,' she says.

'I didn't just want to make paintings, I wanted to put out a message. It was then that my father asked me to draw the story of Buddha in the Madhubani art form. I then began reading more books about Buddha and slowly made almost thirty Madhubani paintings around this theme.'

These paintings help her cope with her and her community's trauma: 'Everything that is suppressed in my subconscious comes out in these paintings. Many times, when I am painting the struggle of someone or a community, my eyes fill with tears. When I was making a painting about the Hathras case,* I was shivering.'

Malvika copes with her trauma by remaining true to her beliefs. 'I tell my friends too to not internalize their trauma or resist it. I say, "If you internalize it, you will let it win."'

---

* The Hathras case refers to the 2020 incident in Uttar Pradesh, India, where a young Dalit woman was brutally gang-raped and assaulted by four men, leading to her death and sparking nationwide outrage over caste-based violence and women's safety.

'No matter what, don't suppress that voice. Respect yourself and it will bring you clarity about what is right and wrong. Don't question yourself, believe in yourself. Listen to your heart.'

Trauma comes in different forms, but what gets passed down is raw, unresolved pain.

And the key to resolving this pain lies with mothers and daughters. We receive trauma and we pass it on—I know of too many women who are struggling to negotiate their relationships with their mothers because they simply do not know where their mother's pain ends and theirs begin.

Talk to your mothers. Hear their stories. The clue to your life will be hidden somewhere in their stories. And that's the beginning of your journey of self-discovery and healing.

7

Mothers and Daughters

> 'The more a daughter knows the details of her mother's life [. . .] the stronger the daughter.'
>
> —Anita Diamant

My mother has always kept a small diary. She doesn't write much but makes a note of important happenings—comings and goings, important events, and other things of significance to her. On 22 September 2023, my father passed away after suffering for around five years. My mother marked his death with one surreal sentence—a snippet of a Tagore song—'*ei akashey amar mukti aloye aloye* [I am now free—I am now eternal, I am the light in the sky].' During the toughest times of her life, my mother has always fallen upon the words of Tagore for consolation. When we spoke, I asked her, 'Do you realize how poignant this is?

Your subconscious is happy that he is now free from the pain, but it is also acknowledging your freedom from pain.'

'I never thought about that,' she mused.

Even though my father was unkind to my mother, in his passing, he has left a void that is felt most keenly by my mother, who was the recipient of his unkindness, and me, the recipient of a lot of his love and kindness, who also disappointed him by calling out his abusive behaviour towards my mother.

I do not regret calling him out—I still love him for the father he was. I just regret that we had lost so much of him towards the end that he never got the chance to understand how hurtful his actions were towards my mother. Maybe he wouldn't have changed, but we would have had some conversations.

Now that he is gone, my mother, sister and I speak about him all the time. All of us are united in the fact that we do not glorify him but accept him for the way he was—a flawed husband but also, an extremely lovable father (and father-in-law), son and friend. We talk because we want the trauma to end with us. And so is the trauma that all of us have carried with us through our lives.

I have always been mindful of not passing down my trauma to my son, Che, but I also know from personal experience and anecdotal evidence, that it is not that easy with daughters. Mother–daughter relationships are particularly sensitive, and there's a risk of transferring trauma regardless of whether the mother is biological, adoptive or surrogate. This might be due to women's common experiences in a male-dominated society or because of generational trauma passed down through families. This shared trauma can create a deep and complex bond between mothers and daughters that goes beyond just genetic connection.

Right at the outset, I can tell you that a mother–daughter relationship is complicated. Both my elder sister and I have inherited my mother's trauma from her own mother and her trauma of being in an abusive relationship, but we have dealt with it in very different ways. My sister has always faced conflicts with my mother, whom she blames for more things than one can imagine—something that I understand comes from a place of deep and immense pain. For me, much of my life has been spent protecting my mother from pain—from my father's actions or my sister's hurtful words. I was a mother many years before I gave birth and now I know that protecting my mother is always going to be my first instinct.

Is that healthy? No, of course not! But I really do not know of another way of being. Therapy taught me to create boundaries with her, but that worked for, like, a week. Our shared trauma binds us in a way that science cannot explain and psychiatry cannot address. But working on this book and interacting with other women has been more than therapeutic for me. We have created a community and a safe space, and just need to expand it so women can heal each other. The burden of trauma that we bear makes this imperative and non-negotiable.

Mridvika's relationship with her mother was possibly written when she was not even born yet. Her grandmother's tumultuous relationship with her younger brother, she believes, has been passed down through the generations to her. 'Her conflict with her brother was not resolved while she was alive. She was afraid of his anger—always trying to contain it by trying to please and appease him. Some of that angst has passed onto my mother and her sister. They operate at different extremes and have very different approaches to confrontation and problem-solving. If something one says triggers the other [and it happens often], they won't talk to each other for weeks and months and I find myself sandwiched between them. Both come and tell me how they are feeling,' Mridvika says. This emotional burden that women carry through their lives is as invisible as their mental load.

She continues, 'Just carrying the burden of how someone else feels has always been on my shoulders. Being part of this for two generations has affected my relationship with my brother. One of us is able to connect at a deep vulnerable level, one is not. If we challenge each other, then it leads to confrontations. I do sometimes wonder if the strife in my grandmother and mother's relationships has been carried into our relationship.'

Trauma passes down from mothers to their babies while the baby is still growing in the womb. This means that a child can start experiencing the effects of trauma really early in life. When a mother goes through traumatic experiences, it can impact her baby through things like stress hormones or changes in the mother's body caused by stress. This can then affect the baby's development, showing how deep and early the effects of trauma can be passed from one generation to the next.[1]

Rachel Yehuda, a professor of psychiatry and neuroscience, in her article titled 'How Parents' Trauma Leaves Biological Traces in Children', recounts her experiences of attending to 187 pregnant women, following the collapse of the Twin Towers of the World Trade Center in September 2001. When the women came in, they were in a state of shock, 'and a colleague asked if I could help diagnose and monitor them. They were at risk of developing post-traumatic stress disorder or PTSD—experiencing flashbacks, nightmares, emotional numbness or other psychiatric symptoms for years afterwards. And were the fetuses at risk?'[2]

Yehuda's research team quickly got to evaluating the women—the women had also been monitored throughout their pregnancies and beyond.

'When the babies were born, they were smaller than usual—the first sign that the trauma of the World Trade Center attack had reached the womb,' she wrote. Nine months after Yehuda's team examined the mothers and the children, they found that most of the women had developed PTSD and that they had 'low levels of the stress-related hormone cortisol, a feature that researchers were coming to associate with the disorder.'

'Surprisingly and disturbingly, the saliva of the nine-month-old babies of the women with PTSD also showed low cortisol. The effect was most prominent in babies whose mothers had been in their third trimester on that fateful day. Just a year earlier, a team I led had reported low cortisol levels in adult children of Holocaust survivors, but we'd assumed that it had something to do with being raised by parents who were suffering from the long-term emotional consequences of severe trauma. Now it looked like trauma could leave a trace in offspring even before they are born,' she concluded.

An article titled 'Understanding The Mother Wound, The Intergenerational Pain Women Inherit' says, 'As women, mothers live in a deeply misogynistic world, and if those toxic messages haven't been worked out of their belief system, they may inadvertently pass down these burdens to their children. This matrilineal pain is sometimes called the mother's wound. The mother wound is a concept that speaks to the generational pain inherited and passed down between grandmothers, mothers, and daughters caused by living in a patriarchal culture that's oppressive toward women.'[3]

'Mother-daughter relationships are the longest, strongest and most complicated relationships within a family unit. Mothers and daughters are invested in the relationship despite how positive or negative it may be. Within this duo, a mother's influence is heavily considered even if it is never mentioned. Knowing that a mother can shape the morals and values of her daughter, it is important to increase communication and seek understanding from one another,' found a study titled 'Exploring the Impact of Generational Trauma on Mother-Daughter Relationships with an Emphasis on the African American Community'.[4]

This complexity in mother–daughter dynamics can often be traced back to the early stages of life, even to the experiences in the mother's womb. The experiences and emotions a mother goes through during pregnancy can affect her child and if it is a daughter, then as they both live through similar situations and challenges in life, their relationship becomes even more complex.

A study found that 'Trauma can leave a chemical mark on a person's genes, which can then be passed down to future generations. This mark doesn't cause a genetic mutation, but it does alter the mechanism by which the gene is expressed. This alteration is not genetic, but epigenetic.'[5]

What are we really passing on to our children? What did we really inherit from our mothers?

We need to examine the family tree and find out where we come from, what trauma defined the generations who came before us, and understand how that is affecting us. And then, we need to be honest with our children—if they are carrying mysterious burdens, they have a right to know. For example, I needed to know of my grandmother's suicide before I found myself emulating her behaviour—not once but twice. The moment I knew about the trauma of my grandmother, I was able to address the trauma that was passed to me through her better. Ignoring the past, hiding it away or pushing it under the carpet will only have harmful effects on our future generations.

Sitara, in her early thirties, for example, could never understand why her mother was so controlling or so emotionally dependent on her. It suffocated her. But when she hit her teens, she realized that her mother's behaviour was modelled on her maternal grandmother's.

'My grandmother had very strict rules for my mother based on cultural norms and expectations of women. My mother struggled with those rules throughout her life. She passed it all down to me—both the said and the unsaid. I was burdened with her expectations and hope. When I was just eight or ten years old, I felt like I was her saviour. And this was my first understanding of her trauma,' she says.

As Sitara became an adult, she began repeating the same patterns as her mother when it came to relationships. 'My mother never stood up to emotional or physical abuse, although she was educated and grew up in a city. When I was in a relationship, I also compromised a lot. One day, I found myself thinking "At least they are not physically hurting me," when I suddenly remembered that I had heard my mother justify the abuse she put up with those identical words. And I was like, "*Shit! I am thinking like her*!" The kind of relationships I built, the way I explored relationships or the way I loved—they were all modelled on the kind of relationship my parents had,' she says.

'I recently adopted a dog, and I realized that the way my mother was dependent on me, especially emotionally, I was developing the same attachment pattern with my dog. But I told myself I know better than to repeat that toxic dependence.'

Sitara remembers being a regular ten-year-old child and maybe talking back to her mother at times. 'Then in the night, she would lie down beside me, sobbing and saying that I was no different than the others in her life who did not treat her well. I would see her crying through the night, blaming herself for not doing well in life, for not being a good daughter, wife or mother. Growing up around her, I always felt that it was my duty to keep her happy and never do anything that would upset her.'

It must have been a heavy burden for a child to carry throughout her life, but many daughters do so even now. I have done it too. I carry the burden of my mother's trauma and unhappiness with me at all points in time and feel guilty for not doing enough to make her happy or reduce her burden. I understand and empathize with the burden she carries, but I wish she had sought help for it instead of passing it down to me. The burden of trauma keeps getting heavier the more we pass it down through the generations. It's a ghost that haunts us throughout our lives—you can't see it, you are not even sure if it is there, and yet, you know that it is.

I cope with the trauma by acknowledging the fact that it is present in my life, and accepting that it is not something that I can change overnight—that it is a process that's unlikely to be resolved within a generation. And it is here where I often feel thankful that I don't have a daughter to pass this trauma onto. It's not that I think trauma doesn't pass on to sons, but with daughters, it's just an added burden on top of all the discrimination they must deal with as they grow up.

Sitara's mother now suffers from a variety of physical ailments and while she knows it has got nothing to do with her, she still cannot stop blaming herself. 'I have always lived my life on my own terms, and that has upset and disappointed my mother. I do not identify as a woman all the time. I fluctuate in the gender spectrum. I can't stop subconsciously blaming myself or thinking that maybe my choices in life led to her illnesses. My conscious mind knows it's not true, but sometimes, I do give in.' Sitara has been in therapy for over a decade now, which has helped her negotiate her relationship with her mother. 'All through my teens and even in my twenties, I felt disappointed that she could not support me or be there for me. Now, I realize that she could not have become the kind of mother I wanted her to be because she did not have the resources to be so, and I have made my peace with it. Her disappointments with me are as her daughter, so now I interact with her as just another human being—taking away the expectations that come with the mother–daughter dynamic. And, yes, I am not just her daughter—I am also a person in my own right. Accepting this has helped me to not feel guilty for disappointing her with my choices.'

I do that too. I try to look at my mother as a woman—rather than as just my mother—to separate our relationship from the expectations that come with these relationship tags. When I look at my mother as a woman, I only find empathy.

One of Sitara's choices that deepened her mother's disappointment, was her decision to not have children of her own. But Sitara remains determined.

'This chain of sadness and disappointment, this cycle of mother–daughter toxic interdependence ends with me,' she says.

But there are some precious moments, too. 'Sometimes, when it's just her, and me and my sisters, and there's no men present, we all become just women without any relationship tags. We take walks or lie down on the grass and just be ourselves without the expectations that society imposes on us.'

And it is these society-dictated rules that make us sometimes resent our mothers. We grow up with the idea that our mothers are going to be ever-present for us and when that equation changes, it creates rancour.

Tripti, in her mid-twenties, became aware of intergenerational trauma after her father died just after she completed her school education.

'When my father died, I felt this huge rage towards my mother. She was supportive, brought me opportunities that she never had herself and would let me do everything that she was not allowed to do. She never let the scarcity of money come in the way of my dreams, even if it was about taking a swimming class. But she was always emotionally unavailable,' she says.

Tripti's father was abusive towards her mother and yet Tripti could not help feeling sorry for him. She explains, 'Even though I was scared of him, I also could see that he was just a person who saw himself as a failure as compared to his peers.'

'My mother became the provider, both for him and me. He fell sick when I was in fourth standard and died when I was eighteen. Between this time, my mother was completely devoted to him as his primary caregiver,' she remembers. 'My childhood does not come as a memory of deep attachment with my mother emotionally but as someone who always provided for me. It's something very practical.'

And her mother expects her to excel at all times. 'It's exhausting,' Tripti says. 'She doesn't understand the need for rest or leisure because she has constantly been working and taking care of people. If I need a break and tell her so, she just brushes it away and pushes me to carry on. I feel bad for her at first, and then I feel angry—it's a vicious cycle.'

She is scared that she will also put the burden of her expectations on her child. 'I worry that I might end up placing the same kind of pressure on my own child if I choose to have one,' she says. 'Right now, I'm actively working on unlearning these patterns I've picked up from her. I'm also trying to have open conversations with my mom to help her see things from my perspective.'

In Tripti's eyes, her mother's insistence on self-reliance was a survival tactic, a way to ensure that she—her mother—had an identity separate from her husband's, because, in a world where no one else seemed willing to help, that identity was all she had to hold onto.

Tripti remembers when she was just four years old, a time when her father had suffered his first heart attack, her mother had sat her down and told her that no matter what happened, she needed to be prepared to take control of her own life. Her mother was forever preparing herself for the next disaster, the next misfortune that would strike her, and sometimes, Tripti wished she would just let go, lower her guard and be free from the cycle of worry and anxiety that seemed to rule her every waking hour.

'We talk more now than we did before. She doesn't dismiss my points of view, but listens and tries to understand where I am coming from. Emotional conversations with her are still very difficult, but we are working on it,' she tells me.

'Growing up is also about this strange acknowledgement that we have become like our mothers. Maybe because my ideas of her are evolving, I understand the context of her life better now. As a feminist, I was always angry with her for giving into patriarchal structures but now, I realize that she always had her own aspirations and that, in her own way, she was pushing at those structures,' she says.

'When I was home last, I told her that "Sometimes you can just walk and not have a destination." She would always go out of the house for a purpose. As a child, whenever I would go out, I was told where to go and when to come back. One day I went back home and told her about going to a place where I was told never to go. I said, "See, I came back home safe and did not die." This changed something in her. She would then go to some nearby place where she had never gone before and tell me about that experience over a call. That is something that I really cherish,' Tripti says.

Our mothers are also often our protectors, especially against patriarchal forces. We look towards them for direction, for the strength to speak up and for the courage to stand our ground. But when that doesn't happen, when we feel they have sided with patriarchy, the feeling of having been let down, of being betrayed, can cut very deep.

Akruti, in her mid-twenties, was disappointed with her mother the day her father hit her brutally for not cleaning her room. Her mother just stood there and stopped her from calling the police, as she was worried that her father would lose his job and there wouldn't be anyone to support the family financially. Something changed in their relationship that day. And she spent a long time hating her mother. 'But you cannot really talk about it—it is not okay to hate your mother,' she says. 'So, the resentment kept building within me.'

Akruti has also consciously tried to stop herself from repeating her mother's patterns in relationships. 'It is tough,' she says. 'I find it very difficult to say no but I also do not want to show love as my mother did—I know where it leads to. So, I struggle with that a lot in my romantic relationships.' And when she said no, she faced isolation and alienation from her closest friends. 'I think it is the fear of being left out by the people around us that makes it very difficult for women to say no to something—mostly in friendships and intimate relationships.'

Their relationship began to improve, ironically, at a time of great emotional upheaval in her mother's life—when she caught her husband cheating on her with another woman. Akruti knew too, having caught her father spending time with the other woman. While tiptoeing around the topic, the two ended up connecting in a way they had never connected before. 'My mother would never talk to me about her sadness, but I knew. And she knew that I knew, and there was no going back from that,' she says. 'She started opening up to me about things after that. We would talk about relationships, people, emotions. She even planned my birthday at home with my friends and invited my boyfriend. She was like a new person. Until she died, we were in the best phase of our relationship where we were emotionally connected as confidantes. It was around the time she also decided to divorce my father.'

But life had other plans—just when she was finding herself and fixing her relationship with her daughter, Akruti's mother died.

'Two years ago, when she passed away, I started revisiting my memories of her. It was like I was seeing her with new eyes. It hurts that I lost my mother just when I found her,' she says.

In 'Mothers and Daughters . . . It's Complicated', Donna L. Roberts writes: 'The mother-daughter relationship, one of the most profound and dynamic bonds in human society, is a labyrinth of complex emotions, shared experiences, mutual learning, and intense love. This relationship often oscillates between extremes, from friendship to rivalry, from camaraderie to tension. Yet, despite the complexities, it is a bond that remains unbroken, growing stronger and more nuanced with time.'

Given the intense feelings and complexities involved, it's unsurprising that this relationship can have a big impact on mental health. The deep emotions and changing dynamics between mothers and daughters can really affect how they feel and think.

Shubha's struggles with anxiety and depression began in 2021 when she was busy preparing for her UPSC exams. 'I couldn't focus on my studies,' she says. She was finally diagnosed with severe depression after three months. It was at that time that she also came to know the source of her depression, its connection with her mother, and the family system she grew up in. She was diagnosed as a 'parentified' daughter—when the daughter plays the role of the mother for her own mother. Family systems theorist Salvador Minuchin coined the term 'parentification' in 1967 when he noticed that parents sometimes end up giving their kids the roles that are really meant for adults, like taking care of other family members. Psychologist Ivan Boszormenyi-Nagy further broadened the definition to point out that when there's an unfair balance in a family—like when kids are doing more giving and helping than receiving—it can lead to serious problems for the child. Nivida Chandra, a New Delhi-based psychologist and researcher, had written in 'Were You A "Parentified Child?" What Happens When Children Have to Behave like Adults', about parentified children that 'these children developed a way of intuiting how to support their parents and others. This was necessary for their own psychological survival. Not caring for their parents was not an option. The consequences could range from the parents withholding love from the children to outright violence between the parents themselves, and the child would then blame herself. These children do not have the opportunity to understand that the problems they are trying to solve are not their own, or why the problems continue despite their best efforts. They learn only that they need to pay more attention, intuit better.'[6]

Parentification between mothers and daughters is frequent in patriarchal cultures. Life coach Bethany Webster, who works with the concept of the 'mother wound', pain rooted in mother-daughter relationships that are passed from generation to generation in patriarchal cultures, wrote in her blog post, 'Parentified Daughters as Adults: Mother Yourself' that 'Often a parentified daughter must grow up very fast and loses the chance to be a child, as she is expected to manage the emotional and/or physical needs of her mother and/or father. This kind of dynamic sets up the daughter for low self-esteem, poor boundaries, a deep sense of shame and co-dependent relationships. Often these daughters grow up to be high achievers and/or emotional caretakers (among other patterns). Major challenges for these women can be self-care, self-compassion and self-love.'

Shubha's experience of parentification had left her confused and frustrated.

'In terms of our relationship, I am the mother, but when it comes to making decisions, I don't have the power. I can voice my concerns but not make decisions. My mother was subjected to this very pattern as a child and she just passed it on to me,' she continues. 'It's a toxic cycle. If I don't break it, it will pass onto my offspring.'

'I tried to understand how my mother became the person she became through her relationships with her own mother and then her husband, my father. My father was mostly absent so my mother had to harness her masculine energy—she was the one who ensured that my siblings and I had a good education. She was always at odds with her feminine energy because she thought it made her weak.'

Shubha has struggled with feelings of anger and resentment against her mother, but through all of that, she also found the courage to start telling her mother right from wrong. 'I come from an upper-caste family. I have always seen separate utensils being kept for so-called lower-caste visitors or workers. I could not call her out earlier, but today, I have been able to separate my personality from her and can be more honest without fearing that I am hurting her. I am still in the process of mentally detaching myself from her. But my reactions to her come from a place of empathy now.'

She agrees that she is like her mother in some respects and says, 'My mother would not go to the hospital unless her health was very bad, something I have also inherited. I find myself in a difficult position when it comes to doing things for myself but I am working on it.'

When Shubha was younger, she was abused by a male relative. When she confided in her mother, she promised to talk to him but never did. The next morning I saw them talking to the same person as if nothing had happened. My parents became enablers,' she says. 'I felt betrayed.'

Her mother is, however, also trying to do better by her. Recently, when Shubha wanted to discuss her abuse, her mother listened to her and apologized. 'That was a good moment,' she says.

Sometimes, as my friend, Uma,* says, we not just inherit our mother's trauma but also their pain and disappointments, fears and anxieties. Uma is talking about the broader emotional legacy that mothers pass down to daughters. It's an interesting aspect of emotional inheritance between generations because while pain, disappointment, anxiety and fears can exist independently outside of trauma, they often emerge from everyday sources. The disappointments and unfulfilled dreams of our mothers, their fears and anxieties might not be actual trauma, but they can still significantly affect us.

It affected Uma too. 'For the longest time, I couldn't separate my ambitions from hers or my pain from hers. For example, my sense of justice or injustice—is that mine or hers? I don't know. A lot of things that I hadn't even processed, I'd already taken in. I inherited her low self-confidence and self-doubt. I inherited her reluctance to be dependent on a man or anyone else

* Name changed.

and believed that we must only rely on ourselves. I inherited her distrust of the world and for the longest time, I didn't know that distrust was not mine.'

It took Uma a long time to identify this and address it. 'I can relax sometimes—now that I am able to tell the difference between what's mine and what I inherited.'

Uma says that when she became a mother and began to give her child her perspectives, she suddenly realized that she had become someone 'who didn't want to be seen or heard and was holding back all the time' because she didn't trust that the world would accept her for who she was. It struck her with immense clarity that this was not her world view, but something she had inherited from her mother. 'These were not my fears but my mother's and I was carrying them along as my own,' she says. 'It took me some time to unlearn everything that I was carrying around; to accept that I was not my mother and to let go of all those fears that were holding me back.'

Separating our own experiences from those of our mothers involves considerable conscious effort because along with inheriting their pain, trauma and struggles, we also carry with us an innate empathy for our mothers. As daughters, we deeply feel and often internalize our mothers' various struggles and unhappiness, whether these occur at home or in the outside world. This sense of empathy comes from the knowledge that this possibly is going to be our future—because when it comes to women, the more things change, the more they remain the same. This often leads us to feel a strong sense of responsibility for our mothers' happiness. We might find ourselves trying to fix their problems or sacrifice our own needs to ensure their well-being. This dynamic, while rooted in love and empathy, can create a complex interplay of emotions where our own identity and experiences become intertwined with those of our mothers. I have been trapped in this complex interplay of emotions throughout my life. I have felt immense happiness when my actions or decisions have made my mother smile—because, as far as I could see, no one else was bothering to try. No one cared whether she smiled or if her smile was forced; no one cared if she wanted to sleep rather than serving ten unexpected guests or how everyday gendered slights made her wince—nobody possibly looked at her long enough to care. But after a while, I will admit that making her happy became untenable for me because her fears and insecurities started pressing down on me. I felt repressed and at odds with the world. It was at that time that I started setting boundaries—where her trauma ends, my freedom begins. But this freedom did not come without guilt. In the end, trauma has to end somewhere and we are the only ones who can make it stop, the only ones who can break the cycle. So, I did. For myself, and for my mother.

Uma once told me that who we are is often determined by who our ancestors were. Her ancestors were farmers, and in farmer families, women are used to working hard at home and in the fields. Women farmers labour hard to cook and clean while doing manual labour on their land and looking after livestock as well. 'My mother was a keen reader but her basic instinct was always of a farmer woman,' she says. Which means, she felt compelled to take care of everything herself without expecting help from anyone else. But that works out very differently in the cities. 'When you're working on farms, you're actually working away a lot of your stress because of the physical labour. A lot of emotions get processed in that—in the singing, in the walking, in the being in the mud and in the hard work that you do. You sleep well at night,' she says. But in the cities, people are islands—the work is more mental than manual and women end up living in their heads a lot. You become more guarded. And then you pass it on to your daughters. That happened to Uma too. So, when she reached her teenage, she started pulling away from her mother. 'I realized that the way she was holding herself back, she was holding me back also, from a lot of things. There were fears that I could see were irrational and holding me back. So, there came a time when I was just running away because I didn't want to be like her—I wanted to trust and love without fear and explore the world. Once I figured myself out, I was okay. Then I went back to her to rekindle that bond. It's a full circle and we've come back to each other—each better for the experience of the distance.'

And perhaps, ready to put themselves first.

8

Be the First One on Your To-Do List

'Women in particular need to keep an eye on their physical and mental health, because if we're scurrying to and from appointments and errands, we don't have a lot of time to take care of ourselves. We need to do a better job of putting ourselves higher on our own to-do list.'

—Michelle Obama

When Priya's daughter was diagnosed with dyslexia in 2005, her husband decided to ignore the diagnosis, quite certain that, as usual, Priya would comply with his decision. But Priya was not the old Priya any more—something had changed and some things were still changing inside her. Her metamorphosis was underway and she was in no mood to go back to being the doormat that her spouse and his family had reduced her to over the years. 'My inability to put myself first was starting to trickle down into decisions about my children's well-being,' she says. 'This was when I decided to take back control. I refused to turn a blind eye to my daughter's diagnosis and put her in therapy.'

A few later years, when her husband, who was almost always in between jobs, got a job and started pressing her to quit hers, she flatly refused. 'I stood my ground because I realized it took me a long time to get back control over my own life and if I left my job, I would be giving it back to him on a platter,' she says.

The process that began in 2005 finally ended in 2012 when she walked out of her marriage.

'I am in complete control of my life now and it feels so, so good. When I moved away to a different city after my divorce, I felt truly free. My children are grown up now, ready to go abroad for their higher studies; I am doing well in my career and people respect me for the professional I am, not because I am a woman in STEM or a single parent. I am valued as a professional. It makes me happy.'

Taking back control also means controlling your own money.

Yes, money changes a lot of equations, which is why men like to control women's money—one way of doing this is by convincing (gaslighting) women that they are bad with money and that they cannot be trusted to save and not spend.

According to the Pew Research Centre in 2023, American women 'typically earned 82 cents for every dollar earned by men'.[1] This was almost the same as in 2002 when they earned 80 cents on the dollar. In India, men earn INR 12,048 ($145) per month on average, while women earn INR 8,034 ($97).[2]

The income gap shows that we may talk about removing barriers to women's economic participation, but in reality, the barriers are either not moving or are giving way to new barriers that are coming up in their place. It's an indictment of our governments that women are still earning less than men, and that, owing to structural and systemic barriers associated with their reproductive roles, they are stuck in limbo when it comes to earning money. Take for example, young mothers—in 2022, 70 per cent of mothers in the US (ages 25–34) had a job or were looking for one, compared to 84 per cent of women of the same age without children at home. 'This amounted to the withdrawal of 1.4 million younger mothers from the workforce. Moreover, when they are employed, younger mothers tend to put in a shorter workweek—by two hours per week, on average—than other women their age. Reduced engagement with the workplace among younger mothers is also a long-running phenomenon,' the Pew Research found. In the US, 1.4 million women are missing from the workforce—in India, according to the first-time use survey, only 20.6 per cent of women aged between 15–59 years were engaged in paid work as compared to 70 per cent of men in the same age bracket. But when it comes to unpaid care work—94 per cent of women and only 49 per cent of all men surveyed aged 15–59 years participated in unpaid work.[3]

To save money, one has to first earn money. Thanks to low access to education or decent employment opportunities, and other patriarchal machinations such as the burden of unpaid caregiving, women are either not working or working in low-paid jobs, mostly in the informal sector.

The New York Life's 2023 Wealth Watch survey found that in 2022, women on average saved just $3,146 (Rs 2,61,118) annually compared to the $7,007 (Rs 5,81,581) saved by men.[4] But it is not because women spend all their money on 'makeup and clothes and jewellery', as the gender stereotyping would have you believe, but because of the simple reason that they are paid less than men. Women save less than men because they have less money or earn less than men, even sometimes for jobs of equal value.

Women's income also decreases owing to what is known as the motherhood penalty or the setbacks that many women face in their jobs and earnings after they become moms. When women have kids, they often end up making less money than women who don't have children or their male colleagues. They pay this penalty by not being considered for promotions or more responsibilities as they are seen as not as committed. Additionally, women who take career breaks after their pregnancies find it immensely difficult to get back into the workforce because of this same prejudice.

There's more to this penalty though. When companies offer flexible hours or the chance to work from home, moms who use these options might be seen as not serious about their careers. These reduced earnings and biased career developments affect their financial stability, savings for retirement and total earnings over time. Childbearing benefits society at large and yet women are financially penalized for having children.[5]

'For women, the biggest challenge is balance. How do you balance your ambition, your family's well-being and your well-being? With men, they are not that worried about family well-being because they perceive their role mainly as a financial provider,' says Saloni. 'When my children were small, I consciously chose to work fewer hours so that I could be a hands-on mother. I was clear that I would build my practice slowly. When they were eight or nine, only then did I start working more hours.'

Women also loathe to have money conversations—to this day, when someone has asked me about my expected take-home salary, I don't think I have ever given a straight answer. But what I have learnt over the years is also that I should not give a straight answer—organizations often have different pay packets for men and women, and if you quote a lower figure (which most women do), they will not say 'Oh but we had more money for this position', they will be happy to offer you what you quoted. So, nowadays, I always ask 'What's your budget for this position?'

This is also true when asking for a raise or a better salary during recruitment—because women's labour has always been so undervalued that it has systematically ruined their sense of worth. When I was offered my first job, the salary that was offered to me sounded very low but I accepted it anyway. Much later, while talking about salaries with a colleague at the same level, I realized he was making almost double what I was making. 'You didn't negotiate?' he asked me. No, I didn't. I didn't realize you could negotiate salaries. My entire fear was that if I negotiated, they might take back the job offer, and after a year-long search for a job, I was eager to just get started. And of course, all these fears are linked deeply with our insecurities, but the fact that decent job opportunities are hard to come by also matters.

'We need to start talking about money,' says Shalaka. 'Because women are usually told not to discuss salaries and talk about money.'

'It is true that not everyone is confident in managing their money. But that's because they have been kept away from money for so long. They never had the power to make decisions in terms of money saving or investing,' she adds.

Men often joke about handing over their salaries to their wives, but are they also handing over the decision-making powers with it? Money, in itself, is just a wad of notes that can buy you stuff, but when that money allows you to make decisions, that's when it gives you power. Men, and our society at large, have made women's relationship with money a joke—women splurge; they don't know how to count, invest or play in the share market; they are spendthrifts and so many other stereotypes—just to keep women away from the power of money. I talked about this extensively in my previous book—how when women work, in many families, it is still the rule that they will hand over their salaries to their husbands, who will then give them a monthly allowance.

'Educating women in terms of investment is essential. When I started earning, I was earning extremely well and yet, I was not ready to risk my money through stocks because I was not educated enough on how or when to do it. Women have taken the easy way out when it comes to managing money but that needs to change,' says Shalaka.

Men also do not always manage their own money—they outsource it to wealth managers. Women can do the same. For example, many women have no clue about filing taxes and let their partners do it for them. The men are not doing it themselves either—they are hiring a chartered accountant to do it for them. Women can do that too. But most women have been socialized to believe that even if they earn money, it is a man's job to manage it. This particular socialization runs so deep that most women do not think twice about handing control to their husbands. Recently, during a conversation about managing money with my friend, Dina,* we started talking about filing for taxes every year and she told me that her ex-husband has been pestering her to let him do her taxes—like he used to when they were married. She was furious and wanted to get in touch with my accountant to file her taxes. But before she could even get in touch with the accountant, her ex-husband had gone into her account and filed the

* Name changed.

taxes for her. Indian men have no boundaries and their sense of entitlement is unmatched—add to that the fact that women have been brought up to give them control of their lives, and you have a vicious cycle. Dina had blocked his phone numbers and his accounts on social media but had completely forgotten that he still had control over some crucial financial aspects of her life. Financial understanding and awareness have to begin in schools. Women need to be taught about money and savings from their school days. Because, like it or not, money is power. It is also precisely why women have been gaslighted for centuries about being bad at math and numbers, told that they should let the men handle the money.

Having a joint bank account or letting them do your taxes are just different subtle ways in which women are made to depend and keep depending on men under the guise of love. Because when women become truly independent, many walk out of the marriages they find themselves stuck in out of sheer dependence.

'I grew up watching my mother managing her own money. She knew what to do with her money and how to invest. She had the financial acumen and she passed it onto me,' said Mridvika. 'I manage my transactions. I don't follow equity investments like the stock market, but I manage other investments on my own, based on some mutual consultation with my spouse because, you know, our financial goals and goals as a family need to be accounted for. We have a joint bank account for monthly household expenses but the rest we manage individually. And we manage our investments, both of us.'

Mridvika's maternal grandmother too was a wonderful money manager. 'She taught neighbourhood children, earned her own money and contributed to the household income. She passed this down to her children, including my mother. It's denigrating to say that women can't manage money or that for them, money only means shopping.'

When women start earning, their first investments are always in the house or their families. They don't immediately run out to buy a car or a phone like a man. And this is not just a loose statement—there's solid backing for it. According to the United Nations, when women work, they invest 90 per cent of their income back into their families compared to 35 per cent for men.[6]

Many of Saloni's clients say that they don't understand finances, which is why they let their partners deal with it. 'But they don't realize they are handing over a large chunk of control to their partners by withdrawing from financial decisions,' she says. 'When women say they don't understand finances, what they are saying is that they have been socialized to believe they are bad with money.' Women are indeed socialized to believe that even if they do earn, they must hand over the responsibility of managing the money to their husbands. But the subtext is that money is control, money is power—so hand it right back to where it belongs—to the man.

'What happens when something happens to their partners? I ask them these hard-hitting questions to make them aware of how this can impact their lives. They need to know about finances so that they have complete control over their lives,' Saloni says. 'Today there's nothing that we can't learn or teach ourselves. There are free resources and tutorials all over the internet. You just need to believe that if you are capable of earning money, then you are also capable of managing your money,' she says.

'Money means freedom—it means I can retire early, I can travel and I can buy my things. It means I can do with it whatever I want,' says Ira, a woman in her early forties, who works as a vice president at a reputed international bank. 'As women realize that, they are actively trying to learn about money. I have seen this shift in the last 5–7 years.'

My mother always handed over her salary to my father, but she did have her own savings accounts alongside—some of which my father didn't know about. Whenever she had some extra money, she would just put it in a fixed deposit for either my sister or me, or for herself. It was her financial foresight that meant that, after they retired and through my father's years-long illness, they were comfortable financially. My mother-in-law managed not just her own money but all of our money. She was our wealth manager—and what a brilliant mind she had for savings and investments! Although she was risk-averse, she grew her money with sharp acumen, with the help of a wealth manager. I was inspired both by her and my mother and have always managed my own money. I do consult my partner from time to time as he has inherited his mother's financial acumen, while I am more my father's daughter and love spending on my loved ones. But, then again, I am my mother's daughter, too, when it comes to not letting anyone exploit me for my money. My father was exploited a lot for his generosity and mostly by his own extended family.

'Money is extremely important,' says Amu,* a young doctoral student. 'I realized this quite late in my life and I am still paying the price. Women being bad with money is, of course, a myth propagated to control them. So that even those of us who earn have no claim over our earnings.'

Nasreen, an advocate, believed in the stereotype too. 'I considered myself to be bad with money simply because I have a fear of numbers. However, I proved myself wrong when some of my mutual fund investments yielded good profits. Today, I'm about to send my daughter to study at a university of her choice in the UK and to pursue an uncommon career despite all the resistance at home. And I'm able to do that because I'm not turning to anyone to help me with the funds or anything else. It's my money. I have managed it well.'

Taking back control also means addressing the imposter syndrome that doggedly pursues us throughout our lives. *You are here because of all that diversity and gender lark* . . . is the subtext that only women (and the marginalized) can hear.

---

* Name changed.

Men are born with their values and worth predetermined—*he is the protector and the provider. He hunts, he gathers. Family is because he is*. While our understanding of family has evolved over the years, and the concept of the *alpha male* or the *hunter-gatherer* is considered archaic and has no place in modern society or mindset, patriarchy is still propagating these ideas by gaslighting women to believe that they are worthless without a man to protect them and taking away their control over their own lives.

Priya's imposter syndrome made her work way harder than her male colleagues. It was never enough for her that she had broken many barriers to succeed in a male-dominated industry. She had held down a STEM job for her entire career when studies, such as Nadiya A. Fouad's 'Leaning In, but Getting Pushed Back (and Out)', showed that, over the last two decades, around 40 per cent of women who qualified as engineers left or never worked as engineers. That number, according to Fouad's study, has not changed significantly in the last two decades—one in four women leave engineering specifically after the age of thirty, compared to one in ten men.[7]

'When I talk to women, I tell them that they don't have to be 100 per cent always,' says Natasha. 'Women are often raised with the belief that their good qualities and hard work will be recognized automatically, but the reality is we need to be more proactive in showcasing our abilities. In my corporate environment, I actively encourage this. I advise more experienced women to pay special attention to the younger women in the workplace and ensure their voices are heard. I emphasize the importance of revisiting and reinforcing their points, especially after meetings or discussions.'

Even if a woman is not a part of her organization but Natasha notices that she's being side-lined, she makes it a point to pull her aside and remind her of the importance of reiterating her ideas and making her presence felt. 'Creating allies in the workplace can help amplify voices that might otherwise go unheard,' she says, adding that, 'women supporting and empowering each other is not a mere slogan—it has to become an integral part of women's unique work culture.'

'I think the biggest impostor syndrome comes from social media,' says Nidhi. 'Everyone is putting out their biggest achievements, their best pictures, all of that. I suffer from impostor syndrome a lot—especially, you know, when one gets to hear all of these things like I said, the personal updates, the professional updates. All of this puts so much pressure on me.'

For Nidhi, the way out of this maze of unhappiness is to stay honest and true to her real self. She shares without holding back and retains her true self online too. 'Imposter syndrome makes you feel like the more you learn, the more you should doubt your own knowledge. I remind myself that this feeling is influenced by external factors and is not an accurate self-evaluation. So, I try to detach from those feelings and focus on my tasks,' she says.

For Mridvika, impostor syndrome manifests itself in different ways. 'At times, this feeling arises when I compare myself to others, especially in my current entrepreneurial journey. It's hard not to notice that some of my peers, who started with me in business school, are thriving while I'm struggling to figure out how to cover my employees' salaries and bills. This comparison can be demotivating.'

But then Mridvika will have a chance conversation, where she would be asked to talk about her work and why she is doing what she is doing, and the feeling of not being adequate would disperse and she would believe again that her work is 'relevant and useful, and that it will contribute towards building a gender-equal world.' In an ideal world, we should not need those validations. But in this world, we do. As we learn to talk to each other honestly and call out the invisible shackles of our lives that are holding us back, probably way more strongly than the visible ones, we will also need these validations less and less.

For Mridvika, that can only happen when we share our stories. 'Stories are what people remember,' she tells me. 'So tell your story. Don't hold back. Share your story so that other women can feel less lonely and understand that they are not alone.'

Motherhood is idealized way too much in many cultures. The picture that is painted for women is that of a naturally fulfilling and joyful experience. This picture, however, often glosses over the challenges, struggles and moments of doubt that come with it, creating a significant gap between expectations and reality. Most of us walk blindly into this phase of our lives. I, for one, have never glossed over the trials and tribulations of motherhood, and have always said that it's a mixed bag—there are good days, bad days and then, there are very, very bad days.

Mothers are expected to seamlessly adapt to their new role, often with little acknowledgement of the emotional, physical and psychological adjustments it requires. And because we don't talk about the not-so-beautiful aspects of motherhood, many women feel like complete failures while struggling to fit into this new role. Popular culture doesn't help us either—mothers are consistently portrayed as always patient, nurturing and organized, managing their responsibilities with ease. Honestly, short video platforms like Instagram (Reels) and YouTube (Shorts) have done more to demystify motherhood than many institutional efforts (*aside: from what institutional efforts?*). Through these mediums, women are peeling back the layers of what's long been considered a mystified aspect of life. Now, we're seeing portrayals of mothers as real, multifaceted humans. These social media channels have opened a space for women to frankly discuss often-overlooked emotions tied to motherhood, like frustration and anger.

But it is too little, too late for many of us, who have already internalized these 'good mother' expectations and often find ourselves forever lacking.

I remember when I became a mother and my son was handed over to me for the first time, I expected to feel this rush of motherly love wash over me—as popular movies and works of literature say it does—and there were . . . crickets. There was wonder. And fear. And guilt that right from the get-go, I was a bad mother. I thought, 'Which mother doesn't feel an instant connection with their child?' As I would learn later, about 20 per cent of new moms and dads feel no real emotional attachment to their newborns in the hours after the delivery. 'Sometimes, it takes weeks or even months to feel that attachment. If you haven't begun bonding with your baby, don't feel anxious or guilty—it should come with time,' says WebMD. 'Bonding can be especially difficult if you had a C-section or couldn't see your baby right after the birth. It can also be difficult if your baby was premature and had to spend time in the neonatal intensive care unit (NICU), or if you adopted the child. It may take longer to bond in these instances, but it eventually should happen.[8]

'Some mothers develop postpartum depression, which prevents them from completely bonding with their babies. The pain and exhaustion from childbirth, especially from a difficult delivery, can also get in the way of the bonding process.'

And yet, everyone from the nurse practitioner to the doctor to the paediatrician and, most often, family members and acquaintances, will make a woman feel like an imposter for not immediately bonding with their newborns.

The nurses at the hospital where I had my C-section were frustrated that I did not already know how to be a mother, how to hold the baby or feed him. And their judgement made me anxious. I felt useless as if I was an imposter. My bond with Che developed over time, away from the prying eyes of society, when it was just him and me and I could show a little courage and pick him up or rock him without someone judging me. I remember our first visit to the paediatrician for his first vaccine when I was so scared of not holding him properly that my heart was thudding. The doctor started screaming at me: 'What kind of a mother are you? You modern girls. You don't even know how to hold a baby the right way.' I should have said, 'Oh, excuse me, doctor! I am sorry my mother thought educating and empowering me would be more important than teaching me how to hold a baby.' But at that point in time, I was distressed and embarrassed. My mother-in-law, who had accompanied us to the doctor, interrupted firmly. 'We have all learnt along the way,' she said to the doctor, with a smile, while also making it clear he was being unreasonable. Not that it mattered to the doctor, who had already made up his mind that because I was a working mother, I was a bad one. This was just the beginning of being shamed for not doing things right for my child. I began to turn a deaf ear to the advice and suggestions that screamed 'You are doing this wrong. You don't know anything. Do better. You are a bad mother.' She counselled me when we were alone with suggestions that were always gentle and always began with 'You have your way, but this is what I found helpful . . .' That helped a lot.

I had once confided in her about feeling like an imposter mother. 'You will be made to feel like an imposter throughout your life,' she told me. 'But you need to know that the people who matter won't make you feel like an imposter. It's always people who don't matter who make you feel that way. But why let those people who do not matter have so much control over your life?' My mother-in-law might sound all sorted out now, but for her, too, it was a process. In their generation, therapy was not something that was easily accessible for women (it still is not—the cost is often prohibitive). So, she found a workaround.

She enrolled herself in a counselling course to learn the nooks and corners of the human mind. 'That really changed the way I was looking at a lot of things, including motherhood,' she would tell me. What I have always taken away from her story is to do what you need to do—for her, it meant giving into love and marriage with a man nine years her junior or having a child at thirty-seven. I am sure she was not immune from the raised eyebrows around her, but she found a way to deal with it because she realized her own well-being was as important as her family's. Women have to do that—do what works for them and find functioning workarounds till they have institutional support to be the people they were always meant to be (equal citizens with equal amounts of work-life-relationship problems without gender coming in the way).

I have also felt like an imposter when I have gone away on work trips for a few days or when I am half-listening to my son when he is excitedly telling me something because I am working on a deadline. These constructs of a woman's reproductive responsibilities must be challenged. A parent is a parent—just because a mother has given birth, it does not make her more responsible for her children.

'As a mother and a daughter, I always thought I was an imposter. I still feel like I was not there for my father and could have done so much more. Even as a mother, that feeling is always there. I feel guilty that I put my kids through fifteen years of living with a toxic parent,' Priya said.

When Priya finally went to therapy, she built up her confidence—not just in her professional life, but also in her personal life—and accepted that there was just parenting and not good or bad parenting.

Priya started therapy in 2013 because she could not sleep as nightmares were keeping her awake. 'I used to have really bad nightmares. I was always anxious. I used to freeze when I had to make decisions.' She was diagnosed soon with post-traumatic stress disorder or PTSD. 'Abusive relationships can do a lot of damage to your emotional health and mental well-being,' according to an article on Healthline. 'They don't just hurt you in the moment. They can destroy your sense of safety, diminish self-confidence and self-worth, and make it difficult to trust anyone else.'[9]

Escaping an abusive relationship doesn't mean the end of the trauma. Many women develop lingering fear or distress. The article mentioned above explains that post-traumatic relationship syndrome (PTRS) is a unique type of trauma that applies to people who have faced abuse in their close relationships—be it physical, sexual or emotional.

The key difference here is that when you've experienced this kind of abuse, you don't necessarily try to forget about it or numb the pain. Instead, you might be stuck reliving those painful memories over and over again. This constant revisiting of the trauma can make it challenging to heal and move forward.

The stress from an abusive relationship manifests a bit differently from typical post-traumatic stress disorder (PTSD). With PTSD, you tend to go back and forth between two states. You have flashbacks and intrusive thoughts that bring the trauma back into your mind, making you feel like you're in the middle of a crisis. As a result, you start avoiding things that could trigger those memories.

However, PTRS doesn't involve the same kind of avoidance seen in PTSD. Instead, you can't escape those memories or reminders of the abusive relationship, and you're fully aware of what happened. Since you can't numb yourself to the pain, you might try to manage your emotional response in various ways.

In PTRS, the trauma comes in overwhelming waves. Survivors often struggle to understand what happened to them—they have difficulties in processing the trauma and the abuse.

So, in a nutshell, PTRS is about how people cope with the ongoing memories and distress from abusive relationships, which is a bit different from how PTSD typically works.

'I should have started therapy earlier—especially when I was still in the marriage. I could have become a better parent and a better person for myself. I could have become much calmer. Calm and composed. When I say have it all, that's what I mean—for me, having it all means switching off the chaos and becoming calm and composed,' Priya says.

And then there's self-worth. Given the structure of our society, women have been in abusive relationships forever—beginning with their parents and perhaps ending with their partners. Sometimes they are overtly violent and perhaps easier to address but often, they fly below the radar.

'Unfortunately one of the common threads amongst women is low self-worth. The reasons are very different, and circumstances are different, but it all boils down to low self-worth. Some of the women I work with as a life coach are CEOs of companies, running their own businesses, super successful but their self-worth is really low,' says Saloni.

'One of my clients, who was self-employed, was going through a very tough time. She was completely lost as her work was not bringing her joy any more. To me, she was this fantastic, awe-inspiring woman with an abundance of talent. But she could not see herself the way I saw her. We did a couple of sessions together and she was part of a group programme. All credit to her that during the programme she began to question some of her own deep-set beliefs, she was very honest with herself and she did the work,' she continues. 'Her transformation was so rewarding for me to watch . . . like, now she is at the place where she owns her art. She is still self-employed but she has also found her groove as an artist. She has gone on to win many awards and has found her zeal for life again, which she was questioning a few years ago. Her transformation was beautiful.'

The existence of low self-worth in women is unsurprising. As Bardoloi said,

> Women were (or are) never treated as full-grown human beings. Love her because she is a daughter or sister or mother. Accept women and human beings—as a person. She has her own desires. She will also make mistakes. Women are not allowed to make mistakes. Women are judged more harshly. Look at the way women are judged when they drive. It is also generational work. It can't change in one generation.

She continues,

> It takes three generations for the changes to show. We are already addressing this by having these conversations. Today there's so much conversation about self-love. Even in small towns, women are going through self-love lessons and they can do that now because of their availability online. Technology has been a game changer—it is changing a lot of equations. Technology is shifting the narrative of good and bad; it is empowering women like nothing else could. It has enabled women to start conversations—with each other and the world.

Even when women are experts in their chosen fields, they are gaslighted by men and their achievements are diminished. 'I have spent all my adult life in a university studying history and culture, but my father and brother will still try and explain complicated phenomena based on some YouTube videos or try and tell me how women are "just biologically designed to take care of children" or that "rapes don't happen in a vacuum" or "anxiety is just your imagination,"' says Preeti,* a college professor. 'Lately, I just nod and keep my distance. I want to correct and debate but I just don't have the physical or mental energy to do it. So I just nod and go to my room.' A woman's whole life and her struggles come out of these patriarchal machinations. Her insecurities, lack of self-worth, confidence, self-belief and self-love are what have kept alive this image of men as superior and hence, all control must be relinquished to them. Calling this out is the only way forward.

'I coach more women on self-love and more men on leadership skills. Women need to be clear about their worth and purpose. The conditioning is so deep that they think all unpaid caregiving is their duty. Even when a woman is working or at home, she feels she is responsible. Women need to ensure they are equal partners without being aggressive. We over-give, are physically and emotionally drained, and then, become aggressive. But what we need to be is assertive,' says Saloni.

Nidhi found a release from the vicious cycle in her life by saying 'yes' more.

'I used to be very tentative—if there was any opportunity, there was also a lot of self-doubt. I was

---

* Name changed.

mostly at home and taking freelance projects. I tried to fit in and figure out where I could do justice, and a lot of second-guessing was happening. But I realized that was somehow counterproductive. I tried instead saying yes to things without overthinking and it actually worked. And suddenly, there I was—from being unsure and tentative, I was adventurous, taking risks, breaking out of my comfort zones,' she says.

For Mridvika, loving yourself means prioritizing your needs and wants over everyone you think you are in service of. 'In service could mean your parents, your spouse, your kids, your in-laws, managing the house or whatever. I have learnt to remove time for myself. Some days, it would manifest in "I don't think I want to figure out what needs to be cooked today, someone else could figure it out," or me lying around reading the whole day. My kids play chess professionally, so, you know, whenever their tournaments are scheduled, I would be the one sitting outside from 9 a.m. to 6 p.m. Now, I have started to take turns with my husband. So, today he is in town and he will be taking them while I plan to do nothing—just sit around, read the newspaper and in the evening, meet up with some former colleagues.'

Mridvika is also more honest in her relationships now. 'I express myself more often with my partner, my kids, my parents, my in-laws—often to say, "This is what I need." Finding that vocabulary and practising it, making sure the conversation is still amiable—these are a few things I have trained my mind to do.'

And finally, the question of being enough or not. Who set the parameters of 'enough'? What does it even mean? I might feel one cup of tea is enough for me while someone else might feel they need a cup on the hour. All levity aside, our idea of being enough also stems from the male idea of being enough—which is, of course, linked to self-confidence. Most men go through life without questioning if they are enough at every step of the way. If they actually asked themselves that question more, they would probably be better fathers, brothers, partners and sons. What men ask of themselves is if they are protective enough or providing for their families enough, which again is patriarchy's gift to them—the need to feel masculine, the need to provide and protect all the time, even when they are not needed to. How can we create an equal society when we bring up boys to be protectors and women to be protected? That's right where the power balance gets skewed in favour of the men and boys. Yes, men are as much victims of patriarchy as women are, but they are victims who have a lot of power and who control a majority of resources in this country. What my heart bleeds for is that despite having so much control over everything, men are still not able to extricate themselves from the impositions of patriarchy because they have so much more to lose than us. Women, on the other hand, lead such disempowered and disenfranchised lives, that with the right push, counselling and institutional support, they can challenge patriarchy. The turning point for gender equality in this country will come not when women learn how to be like men, but when they learn to accept themselves, stop judging themselves through the male gaze, make their own rules, help build cities that cater to their needs, and have workplaces where they are not interlopers but workers with different needs, that, when taken care of, will increase the productivity and profitability of their companies.

We won't have to squeeze into existing spaces or bring our own chairs; instead, the room will be inherently designed for everyone, inclusive and welcoming by default.

I realized in my forties that not only was I enough then, but I had always been enough. It was more that I was not just me—the expectations of family, society, and separately, of my mother, her fears, her pain, her insecurities, had bogged me down so much that I couldn't even see who I was any more, let alone feel that I was enough. But when I look back now, I am amazed and proud of who I was in my teen years, in my twenties, and my thirties—I just wish that I had not wasted all those decades pursuing some goal post that patriarchy kept shifting, and running and running and running after the need to be more.

'I have struggled with this voice in my head which says *I am not enough*. Because the very word "enough" is very relative—enough in relation to what? Your neighbour, your cousin, your sister, whoever you want to compare yourself against or with,' Mridvika says. 'So, I have kind of struggled with that. As a kid of the eighties or nineties, growing up meant you had to be upwardly mobile, from middle class to upper middle class, in terms of financial independence, getting a house, your own vehicle, going out on vacation and whatnot. That is what a successful life means. I think, as I have grown in age and maturity, I have started to question all of this. Everyone has their own trajectory and definition of happiness and success, and being enough is so relative that you can't compare one against the other. When this realization dawned upon me, it was easier to not stay in the rat race or compare myself with someone next door. I have struggled with the feeling of being worthless or imperfect but I have also kind of overcome it now. I have stopped worrying if I am good enough or not. Although sometimes, it comes as a bolt out of the blue, a sudden shooting pain.'

Mridvika had taken her children to volunteer at the Gandhi Ashram in Ahmedabad, Gujarat, for their summer vacation this year. 'I am a bootstrap entrepreneur, that's all I could afford,' she says. After the first day of school following their vacation, they came back home with stories of their friends' vacations abroad. 'And, for a fleeting moment, I felt like I could be doing more for them—but these are fleeting thoughts and eventually go away. All I remember is the strength and resilience and how I am enough.'

Taking back control also means setting meaningful boundaries. Most women find it hard not just to say no, but also to set boundaries in relationships—they put themselves last to accommodate others. Natasha taught her kids the importance of respecting her boundaries by respecting their boundaries. 'When they were younger, I would not demand their time; instead, I would ask if they were free to spend time with me,' she says. 'So, now when I am reading or engrossed in something, they don't demand I drop it all to attend to them. They ask if I am free.'

There was a time, some years ago, when she had come back from a long work trip and her younger son wanted her to drop him off at school. 'I was tired, but I guess every mother feels guilty when they are back from a long work trip so although I was exhausted, I agreed,' she says. 'But my older son intervened and pointed out that I looked tired, and I could just say no and drop him some other day.'

Putting yourself first, saying no, being enough, setting boundaries and living a fulfilled life—all of it is possible. It starts with addressing the trauma that women are born with or live with—the trauma they receive, the trauma they pass on, the trauma they inherit and the trauma they experience. Breaking the cycle of trauma is the key to putting yourself first.

'This is again about mental, emotional and spiritual work. You have to understand that you are doing your best. You have to love and respect yourself,' says Saloni. 'If you don't do that it will trickle down to your children. You are teaching your children not to love themselves as well. It's a double-edged sword. When you feel you are enough, when you are okay with the way you are, your children see and imbibe this too. They also feel they are enough in themselves.'

'If patriarchy lets women feel good about themselves, they would refuse to provide so much free labour. Imagine if you are allowed to feel that you are a good daughter, woman, sister and mother. Women will start saying no a lot more,' Bardoloi says. 'Our whole society is geared towards helping men win—women are just accessories who help them with it through unpaid labour making sure they are comfortable when they are home and that their time is managed well.'

Women are made to feel bad about themselves, their contributions to society and families, and their caregiving contributions are belittled. We keep up a good facade but our lives are hard. In fact, it's not even a facade—this treatment has been normalized so much that it is now something that we have to deal with, and how we deal with it is our problem. And I say we change the way we deal with it. The answer lies not in over-giving to others but in over-giving to ourselves; in loving ourselves enough to know that we are enough and that we are capable of even more.

'Women like me are more physically powerful because of the Y-chromosome in our composition. Those who are born as women do not have that. The heteronormative structure has thus normalized a family structure where the wife is fair and feeble, and the husband is physically powerful. Now if the roles are reversed, if the woman is physically more powerful and the husband is reserved, then that does not fit well into the heteronormative consciousness,' says M. 'Which is why, just like transwomen like me, expressive, opinionated and strong cis-het women too face alienation.' This is why women must be suppressed to remain sidekicks to their male relatives.

We need to start talking about women's lived experiences more—we need to come together in safe and non-judgmental private spaces and share our journeys. More than leaning in, we need to gather together, talk and listen as they do in support groups. This means going beyond just encouraging women to assert themselves in their professional lives and instead focusing on fostering communities where they can openly discuss their journeys in a safe, non-judgmental environment. Such spaces can also act as a resource for practical advice, emotional support and solidarity. Women can learn from each other's coping strategies, share resources and offer encouragement. This collective wisdom and support can be particularly powerful for women who may feel isolated in their personal or professional lives. As Bardoloi says, 'One of the most fundamental things about all humanity is that you want to belong, and belonging becomes easier when we share our experiences and those experiences match. There is great strength in knowing that there are others in your situation too. That's how millions have healed, and how communities heal. That's how women can heal too.'

Yes, we are all hounded by life, the hustle culture and all that, but we still need to make time to build these communities with other women. Otherwise, just like our mothers, we will only be leaving behind questions and no answers.

Women need to come together in simple communities—life-experience-sharing communities and support groups. 'If we all sit together and share our stories, the solution will come from all of our experiences—from the experiences of broken women.

In Bengal, they have this tradition of hanging around in tea shops. It is the famous *adda*,* but it's mostly men. We should have such communities for women too.'

She is right and we don't have to look far for inspiration—these communities exist within our societies, among women who do not have money and for whom these communities are a lifeline. Let's take, for example, the self-help groups (SHGs). 'India's SHG movement has evolved from small savings and credit groups that sought to empower poor rural women, into one of the world's largest institutional platforms of the poor,' according to the World Bank. Today, 67 million Indian women are members of 6 million SHGs. *While these groups are aimed at encouraging women's leadership and economic empowerment at the village level, they have played a broader role in changing societal behaviour.* Studies have found that 'these women's collectives are instrumental in bringing normative and behavioural changes at the individual, family and community levels . . . SHG members come together as pressure groups to persuade, negotiate and motivate families and community members to follow and adopt positive and changed behaviour, which contributes to reduced vulnerabilities for women and girls.' [10] Women-led SHGs are great examples of how women-led communities can help transform normative behaviour.

* A place where people gather for conversation.

Women need to know that they are not alone—that what they feel, and how they act and react are all part of historic socialization. What it is, is a form of systemic abuse, and coming together to fight it is the only way forward. Our backs are already against the wall, where do we go from here but forward?

There are small things that only women can do for each other, certain things that only women can understand without any explanations—this silent solidarity is what we need to harness.

Start by making time for your female friends.

Bardoloi says,

> Female friendships are empathetic, and they don't want anything in return. They are there for you because they love you. I began my work because of my girlfriends. They were my first clients and they have spread the word. Without women, I can't do the work I am doing today.
>
> I held their hands through their marriages, divorces, miscarriages, and the kind of safety I felt with them is inexplicable. I had ten women holding me up telling me I was enough, that I was going to be ok and that I was more beautiful than I could imagine—you need that sometimes in life. In my most vulnerable moments, I feel the safest with my women friends.

And to make time for your friends, you must reclaim your right to leisure. Leisure, believe it or not, is a gender equality issue, because women rarely have access to it, and even when they do, they feel like they must fill it up with something or the other, especially unpaid caregiving. If they are not juggling a thousand things a day, what value do they have in the family system? Take, for example, the word 'lazy' that is often applied to women as a slur. A woman who prioritizes leisure and doesn't mind being lazy is looked upon as a woman who is wanting in womanly qualities, which means that she failed her nurturing quotient and consequently, failed as a woman. An article in 2022 asked a very pertinent question—*'There's a lot of talk about how to achieve gender equality at work, but what about gender inequality in leisure?'*[11]

The article cited a study by Mara Yerkes of Utrecht University and her colleagues, where the authors compare and explain gender differences in the quality of leisure across twenty-five countries.[12] To begin with, the study found stark differences between men's and women's leisure across these countries, where 'countries with more egalitarian role expectations, institutionalized egalitarian norms around divisions of care, and higher bargaining power for women in society create a space in which men and women are more equal in their entitlement to use leisure time to relax and recover.'

'When I don't have anything to do, it bugs me. How come I have so much time? Why do I have so much time? Did I forget to do something?' Priya asks.

There always would be a couple of days every month when I would do nothing. I would just laze around watching television, reading and ordering takeaways.

I would call those days my guilty pleasure. Why? I never knew then. Now that I do, I call it my right. While the journey from 'guilty pleasure' to 'right' was long, it was an important one.

'Doing nothing is such an unnatural state of being for women. Just sitting and gazing and doing nothing is such a guilty pleasure for women.' Bardoloi draws from the experience of her clients when she says that women also feel guilty about resting. 'Women compete how much they are labouring for free. *I stay awake with my son till 3 a.m. for his exams. Then wake up at 6 a.m. to make my husband's lunch box*. Why are you taking pride in unpaid labour and suffering?'

It's because leisure has the connotation of laziness, and lazy women are frowned upon; it's not an attribute that is encouraged. 'Just the other day, my aunt was calling out my cousin for being lazy,' Mridvika says. 'And she was like, "Don't be so lazy—when you are married, your in-laws will taunt my upbringing." We are conditioned to believe that a woman who prioritizes rest time is a lazy, bad woman.'

We live in a world where a basic right like leisure is also gendered, where women have to steal their moments of leisure, where they often have a million minutes in their days and not one to their own names.

But the most important part of putting yourself first and taking back control of your life is to escape toxic relationships, whether at home, work or elsewhere.

Dr Yadav says toxic relationships are of various kinds, but in a nutshell, it is 'being with somebody who is actually stunting your growth'.

'It could be anything from emotional to physical abuse, or even living with a narcissistic individual or a partner who is very critical of who you are,' she adds.

Irrespective of their financial status or their personalities, women tend to hesitate to end toxic relationships because of the practicalities of walking out of those relationships and the fear of being judged by society, but also the inherent patriarchy within all of us that makes women feel responsible for the success or failure of a relationship. While more women are working now and are financially independent, they are still hanging onto toxic relationships because of the ubiquitous fear of 'What will people say?'

'If you are materially equipped to leave a toxic relationship but not mentally, ask yourself what you want and how can you reach there. Try and deconstruct the pressure of social conditioning,' Dr Yadav says.

And finally, spend time with yourself. Honestly, loving your own company is the only self-care a woman needs, because while we are taught that love is a virtue and that we must shower it on everyone around us, often at the cost of ourselves, we are never taught to love ourselves and hence, our own company. A woman who is not scared of being alone is a woman who knows her worth. She is a woman who is not afraid to face up to her demons—address her guilt and emotions. Walking alone is a beautiful rebellion for those who have been taught to interpret being alone as being unloved.

'Often, people keep themselves constantly occupied without even realizing it. However, there comes a point when the inner self starts yearning for attention, and this can manifest in symptoms like stress, anxiety or depression if we continue to ignore our true desires,' says Dr Yadav, adding that while taking time for oneself is crucial, it can be challenging for women when they are faced with the societal expectation of always prioritizing the needs of others. The ideal of the self-sacrificing woman leads to guilt when women do prioritize their well-being. 'To overcome this guilt and truly understand oneself, it all comes down to awareness. How attuned are you to your own needs and desires? Only through this awareness can you truly honour yourself,' says Dr Yadav. 'Whether it's solo travelling, cooking or dining, exploring activities on your own—all of these can be a wonderful way to discover your individuality as a woman. It's a beautiful journey of self-discovery.'

Epilogue

TL:DR (Message to My Younger Self)

'You're braver than you believe, stronger than you seem, and smarter than you think.'

—Winnie the Pooh

Dear thirteen-year-old self,

First and foremost, I still see you—wearing those tent-like clothes, hiding every possible curve in your body, and walking awkwardly yet so fast as if you have a train to catch. I see you trying to hide your body and diminish yourself in public spaces. I see you trying to be the best daughter at home and the best student in school. I see you reading with a torch under your bedsheets at night. I see you escaping to distant lands with your books—I see you. So clearly. And I want you to know that you are enough just as you are. The idea of 'having it all' is a heavy burden to carry, and as time goes by, you'll come to understand that it's more about finding what truly matters to you. Your worth is not defined by society's expectations or norms; it is defined by your self-love and self-acceptance.

As you continue on your journey, remember that self-love and self-value are not destinations but ongoing practices. Embrace the imperfections, for they are what make you uniquely beautiful. Your struggles and triumphs will be the ink on the pages of your life story and will resonate with others who have faced similar challenges.

Don't be afraid to challenge the status quo and speak your truth. Though you still don't know what you will become in the future, don't worry too much about it. Being your future self, I can tell you with confidence that you will reach where you need to—where you want to—but don't forget to be mindful of the journey and enjoy every twist and turn. I was so critical and conscious of the way I looked, the way I spoke, my body, my voice which was not sweet and tinny like most women's, and my broad shoulders and big feet. I always tried to diminish myself—every time I saw a picture of myself, I winced. I still do. But it would do you good to know that now when I go back to you, to who I used to be, I am amazed at how perfect I was. Maybe, my eyes have changed—maybe, experience has taught me to appreciate what was. Don't let that happen to you; don't wait for experience to love yourself or find yourself beautiful and perfect—know that you already are.

There will be moments of doubt and uncertainty but never forget your inner strength. You are a force to be reckoned with, capable of achieving remarkable things. Your resilience will carry you through the toughest of times.

Cherish this journey. Life is not just about the destination; it's about the experiences, the people you meet along the way and the lessons you learn. Embrace every twist and turn, for they will ultimately lead you to a place of self-love, self-acceptance and success beyond your wildest dreams.

Let me share with you what I have learned in my journey:

Set Boundaries: It's essential to establish limits with people in your life. Don't depend too heavily on others for your happiness or well-being. While money can contribute to a comfortable life, it shouldn't be the sole focus. Instead, consider that simple activities like morning walks can have a positive impact on your health.

Be Assertive: Being assertive means expressing your thoughts and needs confidently but respectfully. It's a valuable quality to develop. While assertiveness is positive, being overly aggressive can create problems. Being too passive, on the other hand, can lead to people taking advantage of you. Remember, you're not a doormat or a trash can. With determination and focus, you can accomplish almost anything you set your mind to.

Patience and Passion: Patience is important; sometimes, you have to wait for things to fall into place. It's equally crucial to stay passionate about your work. Don't choose a job solely for the money; consider your passion and interests as well.

Report Abuse: If you ever encounter abusive behaviour, don't tolerate it. Reporting it promptly is essential. Don't fall into the trap of patiently waiting for abusive individuals to change; it's not a virtue to endure mistreatment.

Life Lessons: Life teaches us valuable lessons—time is valuable, timing can make a significant difference, the ability to let go of things is a powerful skill, close friendships are precious, working hard is crucial regardless of immediate results, and sometimes, our best achievements go unnoticed by us.

You're Worth It: Understand that you don't have to prove your worth to anyone. You deserve rest, respect and love simply because you tried your best. Celebrate your efforts and small victories; showing up and giving your all is what truly matters.

Don't Overthink: Allow yourself to figure things out independently without the pressure of societal expectations.

Do Your Best: Always give your best effort in everything you do. Don't doubt whether your best is good enough—it is. Make informed decisions and avoid dwelling on past choices.

Believe in Yourself: Never doubt your capabilities. You have the potential to achieve your goals. Keep moving forward confidently and fearlessly. You are the leader of tomorrow—you just have to believe it.

Self-Investment: Invest in yourself by prioritizing your growth and well-being. Have confidence in your choices and don't let the opinions of others hold you back.

Live Life Fully: Embrace life to the fullest. Make the most of every moment, enjoy new experiences, and create a life that brings you happiness and fulfilment.

And finally, you know how they always tell us to choose our battles? Don't. Don't choose your battles. As a woman, you will need to fight all your battles—small or big. As you grow up, you will internalize many stereotypes and patriarchy-imposed rules of what it means to be a woman. This will fog your ideas about small and big battles. But don't let it. Stay true to yourself and what feels right to you. You are the only one who can decide the magnitude of all the battles that life will throw your way. And let me tell you from where I stand today—you will have to choose all your battles. Don't let anyone tell you otherwise.

When my father died in September 2023, the people around me wanted me to stay behind at home while they performed my father's last rites. I fought that battle and went to the crematorium. Many would say that was a big battle. And then, while there, when they came and asked who would perform the last rites, someone piped up with the name of one of my cousins. A cousin, whose brother had once almost killed my father. When I asked 'Why?', someone told me to let it go and the subtext was *pick your battles*. But no, the forty-six-year-old me knew and knows all battles are important. And I performed my father's last rites—*who if not me?* Yes, I am not my father's son—but I am his child, I am born of him. And this is a right that I would fight for—to be the one to see him off on his final journey.

You must fight all battles because you never know which important battle will slip you by. Choosing your battles is flawed advice, at least for women. So, fight all your battles with the same intensity and passion. And while you are doing that, be mindful that people may try to define you and box you throughout your journey, and they may not allow you to define yourself. It's because they are scared that when you start to define yourself, you will also question the society-approved freedom you have been 'allowed'. And that will be the last shackle on your feet—one that is so slyly hidden that sometimes, we go through life believing that we are free, not realizing that this whole time, we have just been playing a part scripted for us. Take back that control and define yourself at every step of the way.

And hey! Never lose the fight in you.

With love and admiration,
Your forty-seven-year-old self

I also asked women on social media as well as those I interviewed for this book, if they had any messages for their younger selves—it seemed like the right way to end this book. Here's what they said. Many of the names have been changed, and that should tell you how far we still have to go. We are still suppressing our voices and are unable to speak up against our families. That's where all the indoctrination and the harmful socialization starts, and the day we break our silence and openly call out our family systems that are thriving on the oppression of women, we will turn this story around.

'Don't lock yourself into a rigid life plan. Instead, set a general direction and embrace life's surprises. As Douglas Adams said, "You may not go where you intended, but you'll end up where you need to be." Remember that change is a constant. Don't fear it; embrace it. Step out of your comfort zone. Taking calculated risks and trusting your intuition can lead to growth and new opportunities,' says Natasha. 'Never forget your privilege. Question assumptions, engage with diverse perspectives and be open to learn and unlearn, especially internalized biases. You're an introvert in an extroverted world. Embrace your nature, but also let people in—some will hurt you, but the enriching friendships are worth the risk.

'Lastly, understand feminism and be a feminist. It's not about demanding special privileges but striving for gender equity. Challenge stereotypes, advocate for equal rights and don't tolerate misogyny. Feminism is rooted in justice and fairness. Smile often, find joy in small moments, and yes, get that dog.'

'Find your worth—whether it is in your career or personal relationships. Cultivate clarity and articulate what you want clearly and openly,' says Mridvika. 'Prioritize yourself and don't compromise.'

Priya says, 'Chill! You will be happy and everything will work out for you—you are stronger than you realize now.'

'Create opportunities for yourself and if those opportunities don't work out, don't lose heart because you will create more opportunities,' says Nidhi. 'Observe people, talk to them and learn from them. Human knowledge and wisdom are so underrated and yet, we learn the most from them.'

'Start setting boundaries. Don't believe too much in anyone and don't lean too much on anyone,' says Dina.* 'Money does buy happiness and anyone who thinks otherwise has too much of the former and by extension, the latter.'

'Being assertive is a virtue. Being aggressive acts as a protective armour. Being docile is unhealthy because

---

* Name changed.

timid/docile women get trampled all over. Don't go around with an invisible placard that reads "Use Me",' says Piu.* 'You are not a doormat or a dustbin. There's nothing you can't achieve if you set your heart and mind to it.'

'Please don't let your dyslexic brain and the taunts of your stupid teachers who did not know you had learning difficulties keep you from higher education. Keep at it and find means to get qualifications that will keep you self-sufficient,' says Karuna.

'I would tell my younger self to go easier on me, to be patient, and wait for things to happen,' says Sara. 'But also, it's important to keep being passionate about the work I'm doing. So don't fall for a job just because it's good money, it's not everything.'

'Report abusive behaviour at the first instance. "Tolerance," which is taught to girls growing up as it was taught to me and "patience" with the abuser to change their behaviour or for circumstances to change their behaviour, are not virtues,' says Malti.†

'Time is the only god. Timing is everything. Letting go is a superpower. Keep your friends close. Work hard and don't think too much about the result. The best achievements are the ones you will easily forget,' says Nusrat.‡

'You don't have to earn rest, respect or love—you're worth it. You deserve the good things because

---

* Name changed.

† Name changed.

‡ Name changed.

you tried your best. Don't dismiss the fact that you tried—showing up is everything. Celebrate the small wins,' says Kavita.*

'Do your best. Don't worry about whether your best is good enough—it is. Make informed choices, and once you have made them, never look back. Smile. The world is a lovely place,' says Anima.† 'Never let anyone doubt you. Never hold yourself back. You got it in you. Just keep swimming and dive deeper. Be fearless.'

'Invest in yourself, look out for yourself, be more confident and don't give two fucks about others' opinion of you,' says Shruti.‡

* Name changed.
† Name changed.
‡ Name changed.

Acknowledgements

I lost my father when I was in the process of writing this book, and while he was slipping away from us for a while, his death was a jolt, nevertheless. You can never be prepared enough to lose a parent. If I was not born to him, my life perhaps would have followed a very different path.

Despite his traditional and conservative nature, growing up, my father allowed me to spread my wings and live life on my terms. He always reassured me that, no matter what, I could always return home. Our relationship was a complex one—I've never sugar-coated it before, nor will I do so now. Though I had my share of ups and downs with him, often due to his treatment of my mother, our connection was one of love and respect.

In our old neighbourhood, he was affectionately known as *Bhowmickda* by everyone. He had a funny nickname for every family member, mine being *Neri*, a playful twist on my *daak naam* (pet name), Mary. This nickname (which means shaved head in English) stuck because, as family lore has it, they shaved my head when I was about six months old as part of a *mundan* ritual.* He loved to eat and share meals with people, and anyone who visited our home while he was still able to do so left with cherished memories of sumptuous feasts. He was generous to a fault—if you asked for a loan of Rs 500, he'd give you Rs 5000, just in case. I owe my generosity to him, just as I owe my strength, resilience and indomitable spirit to my mother. I can never write an acknowledgement without expressing my gratitude to her. I am who I am because she is who she is.

And, as always, I must acknowledge my late in-laws: Nabarun and Pranati Bhattacharya, and my grandmother-in-law, Mahasweta Devi. Their lives have been a guiding light for my thoughts and actions. My late mother-in-law was my best friend, and I learned a great deal about self-prioritization from her. She left us in 2017 and there are still moments when I instinctively reach for the phone to call her, only to be reminded that it's no longer possible. I also learned a great deal from my late father-in-law, who did not

* The mundan ceremony is a Hindu tradition in which the first lock of a baby's hair is ceremoniously cut. This ceremony is usually performed when the baby is between 1–3 years old and symbolizes the child's growth and spiritual journey.

have a single sexist bone in his body; equality was a fundamental part of his being.

A huge debt of gratitude goes to my partner, Bau, and our son, Che, as well as our beagle companions, Kuttush and Gypsy. They endured my mood swings, tiptoed around me when I was stressed, and gently suggested that I 'take a break'. Che even offered to be my research assistant, while Bau volunteered to transcribe, but I graciously declined, as I am admittedly a bit of a control freak. However, I gladly accepted their offers of hugs, shoulder massages and the generous affection of our furry family members.

I'd like to extend my heartfelt thanks to Aishwarya Raj for her assistance with research and transcriptions, as well as Anwesha Ganguly for her contributions to transcribing audio materials. Both were indeed heaven-sent.

Finally, I want to express my deepest gratitude to everyone at Penguin Random House India for turning this book from a mere pamphlet into a reality. This book was once a mere idea, and even though I knew that someday I'd transform it into a book, Chirag Thakkar made it possible in 2023, and for that, I extend my sincerest thanks. My gratitude to Aparna Abhijit, whose insightful editing helped me fine-tune the manuscript further.

Of course, this note would remain incomplete without acknowledging the countless women who have touched my life in various capacities, whether as friends, acquaintances, family, or even strangers on a train or flight. Your trust and willingness to open up to me have exceeded my wildest expectations.

To my readers who so generously showered praise on my first book and read and recommended it: *You are my community, my tribe.*

Notes

Introduction

1 Sue Townsend, *The Woman Who Went to Bed for a Year* (UK: Penguin, 2012).
2 J. D. Smith, 'The Role of Mothers in Society', *Journal of Family Studies* 15 (3) (2019): 247–60.
3 'Stay-at-Home Moms: The Challenges and Rewards,' *Guardian*, 16 May 2017, https://www.theguardian.com/lifeandstyle/2017/may/16/stay-at-home-moms-challenges-rewards.
4 Vanessa McGrady, 'How Working Moms Make It Work', Mom.com, 3 July 2012, https://mom.com/kids/2806-how-working-moms-make-it-work/#google_vignette.
5 'Using Emotional Intelligence Is a Woman Leader's Secret Weapon', *Forbes*, 2 November 2016, https://www.forbes.com/sites/womensmedia/2016/11/02/using-emotional-intelligence-is-a-woman-leaders-secret-weapon/.

6 'Diversity Wins: How Inclusion Matters', McKinsey & Company, 2020, https://www.mckinsey.com/business-functions/organization/our-insights/diversity-wins-how-inclusion-matters.

7 'The CS Gender 3000: Women in Senior Management', Credit Suisse Research Institute, 2019, https://www.credit-suisse.com/about-us-news/en/articles/media-releases/credit-suisse-gender-3000-report-shows-women-hold-almost-a-quart-202109.html.

8 Jack Zenger and Joseph Folkman, 'Research: Women Are Better Leaders During a Crisis', *Harvard Business Review*, 30 December 2020, https://hbr.org/2020/12/research-women-are-better-leaders-during-a-crisis.

9 'Countries Led by Women Have Fared Better During the Covid-19 Pandemic', *Harvard Business Review*, September 2020, https://hbr.org/2020/09/countries-led-by-women-have-fared-better-during-the-covid-19-pandemic.

10 Gemma Hartley, 'Women Aren't Nags—We're Just Fed Up,', *Harper's Bazaar*, 27 September 2017, https://www.harpersbazaar.com/culture/features/a12063822/emotional-labor-gender-equality/.

11 Allison Daminger, 'The Cognitive Dimension of Household Labor', *American Sociological Review* 84(4) (2019): 609–33, https://journals.sagepub.com/doi/10.1177/0003122419859007.

12 Eileen Fischer and Stephen J. Arnold, 'More Than A Labor of Love: Gender Roles and Christmas Gift Shopping', *Journal of Consumer Research* 17(3) (1990): 333–45.

13 Eir Nolsoe, 'How does Christmas impact people's mental health?', YouGov.co.uk, 18 December 2019, https://yougov.co.uk/health/articles/26954-christmas-harms-mental-health-quarter-brits.

14 'Depressive disorder (depression)', World Health Organisation, 31 March 2023, https://www.who.int/newsroom/fact-sheets/detail/depression.
15 Jennifer Ervin et al., 'Gender differences in the association between unpaid labour and mental health in employed adults: a systematic review', *Lancet Public Health*, September 2022, https://www.thelancet.com/journals/lanpub/article/PIIS2468-2667(22)00160-8/fulltext.
16 'Why Women Are More Prone to Depression', MindSet, https://mindsetsd.com/why-women-are-more-prone-to-depression/, last accessed 24 January 2024.
17 'Stress Effects on the Body', American Psychological Association, 1 November 2018, https://www.apa.org/topics/stress/body.
18 D. S. Lessin and N. T. Pardo, 'The impact of perfectionism on anxiety and depression', *Psychology and Cognition* 2 (1) (2017): 78–82, https://www.researchgate.net/publication/334701977_The_impact_of_perfectionism_on_anxiety_and_depression.
19 'Depression: His Versus Hers', Johns Hopkins Medicine, 22 September 2023, https://www.hopkinsmedicine.org/health/conditions-and-diseases/depression-his-versus-hers.
20 Sarah Thébaud et al., 'Good Housekeeping, Great Expectations: Gender and Housework Norms', *Sociological Methods & Research* 50(3) (2021): 1186–1214.
21 Anu Madgavkar et al., 'The Economic Benefits of Gender Parity', *Stanford Social Innovation Review*, 8 March 2016.
22 Nidhi Sharma, Subho Chakrabarti and Sandeep Grover, 'Gender Differences in Caregiving among Family - Caregivers of People with Mental Illnesses', *World Journal of Psychiatry* 6 (1) (2016): 7–17.
23 'The gender pay gap in the health and care sector: A global analysis in the time of COVID-19,' World Health

Organization and International Labour Organization, 2022, https://www.ilo.org/wcmsp5/groups/public/---dgreports/---dcomm/---publ/documents/publication/wcms_850909.pdf.

24 'The Gender Wage Gap by Occupation, 2019, and by Race and Ethnicity', National Women's Law Center, https://nwlc.org/resources/the-gender-wage-gap-by-occupation-2019-and-by-race-and-ethnicity/, last accessed 10 January 2024.

25 Kristen R. Hamilton and Marc N. Potenza, 'Relations among Delay Discounting, Addictions, and Money Mismanagement: Implications and Future Directions', *American Journal of Drug and Alcohol Abuse*, 38 (1) (2012): 30–42, https://www.ncbi.nlm.nih.gov/pmc/articles/PMC3691101/.

26 Marcus Dittrich and Kristina Leipold, 'Gender Differences in Time Preferences', *Economics Letters* 122 (3) (2014): 413–15.

27 Kevin P. Madore and Anthony D. Wagner, 'Multicosts of Multitasking', *Cerebrum*, 1 April 2019, https://www.ncbi.nlm.nih.gov/pmc/articles/PMC7075496/.

28 Gijsbert Stoet et al., 'Are women better than men at multi-tasking?', *BMC Psychology* 1(1) (2013).

29 Ibid.

30 'Sequential, Concurrent Multitasking Is Equally Hard for Men, Women', ScienceDaily, 19 August 2019, https://www.sciencedaily.com/releases/2019/08/190814144505.htm.

31 'The Harried Life of the Working Mother', Pew Research Center, 1 October 2009, https://www.pewresearch.org/social-trends/2009/10/01/the-harried-life-of-the-working-mother/.

Chapter 1: The Enlightenment: What Women Want

1 Mary Wollstonecraft, *A Vindication of the Rights of Woman* (London: J. Johnson, 1792).

2 Lalitha Dhara, 'Social revolutionary, feminist and poetess Savitribai Phule', 19 December 2016, Forward Press, https://www.forwardpress.in/2016/12/social-revolutionary-feminist-and-poetess-savitribai-phule/.
3 Ada Calhoun, 'The New Midlife Crisis', Oprah.com, https://www.oprah.com/sp/new-midlife-crisis.html, last accessed 24 January 2024.
4 Terri Apter, 'Midlife Women: Why Are They More Assertive?', 11 August 2011, https://www.psychologytoday.com/intl/blog/domestic-intelligence/201108/midlife-women-why-are-they-more-assertive.
5 Claudia Laroye, 'Invisible No More: The Rise of the 50+ Solo Woman Traveler', Adventure.com, 26 January 2023, https://adventure.com/over-50s-solo-women-travelers/.
6 Sanjana Shenoy, 'Study Reveals Older Women Opt For Solo Travelling More Than Others', CurlyTales.com, 26 February 2020, https://curlytales.com/study-reveals-older-woman-opt-for-solo-travelling-more-than-others/.
7 Lucy Plummer, 'Indian Women Are Travelling More Than Ever & Here Are Some Initiatives Helping Them Out', Better India, 17 May 2017, https://www.thebetterindia.com/101166/indian-women-travelling-millennials-trend-solo-groups/.
8 Eshita Gurung, 'The Solo Indian Women Tourist', *International Journal of Research and Analytical Reviews* (IJRAR) 5(4) (2018).

Chapter 2: No Can Do: The Power of Saying No

1 Suzanne Gerber, 'Why Even Strong Women Sometimes Have a Hard Time Saying No', 1 March 2012, Next Avenue, https://www.nextavenue.org/why-even-strong-women-sometimes-have-hard-time-saying-no/.

2 Audre Lorde, *A Burst of Light: And Other Essays* (India: Dover Publications Inc, 2017).
3 Jim Folk, 'Boundaries And Anxiety', Anxietycentre, 16 May 2021, https://www.anxietycentre.com/articles/boundaries-and-anxiety/.
4 '2010 Stress in America: Gender and Stress', American Psychological Association, 2012, https://www.apa.org/news/press/releases/stress/2010/gender-stress.
5 'How Women Who Do It All Can Combat Burnout: How to Beat Burnout and Ask for Help', Cleveland Clinic, 21 April 2021, https://health.clevelandclinic.org/how-women-who-do-it-all-can-combat-burnout.
6 Pushpendra Singh and Falguni Pattanaik, 'Unfolding Unpaid Domestic Work in India: Women's Constraints, Choices, and Career', *Palgrave Communications* 6 (111) (2020).
7 Susan Faludi, *Backlash: The Undeclared War Against American Women* (USA: Crown, 2006).
8 Hannah Riley Bowles, 'Why Women Don't Negotiate Their Job Offers', *Harvard Business Review*, 19 June 2014, https://hbr.org/2014/06/why-women-dont-negotiate-their-job-offers.
9 Jenna Goudreau, 'Why It's Harder For Women To Say 'No' To Extra Work', *Business Insider*, 18 December 2014, https://www.businessinsider.in/why-its-harder-for-women-to-say-no-to-extra-work/articleshow/45555124.cms
10 Suzanne Gerber, 'Why Even Strong Women Sometimes Have a Hard Time Saying No', Next Avenue, 1 March 2012, https://www.nextavenue.org/why-even-strong-women-sometimes-have-hard-time-saying-no/.
11 Kendra Cherry, 'How to Stop People-Pleasing', Verywell Mind, 21 March 2023, https://www.verywellmind.com/how-to-stop-being-a-people-pleaser-5184412.

12 Jamie Ballard, 'Women are more likely than men to say they're a people-pleaser, and many dislike being seen as one', YouGov, 23 August 2022, https://today.yougov.com/society/articles/43498-women-more-likely-men-people-pleasing-poll.

Chapter 3: Redefining Having It All

1 Sheryl Sandberg, *Lean In: Women, Work, and the Will to Lead* (New York: Knopf, 2013).
2 Linda Elizabeth Chardon, 'The Personal, Political, and the Virtual? Redefining Female Success and Empowerment in a Post-feminist Landscape', University of New Hampshire Scholars' Repository, 2013, https://scholars.unh.edu/cgi/viewcontent.cgi?article=1203&context=honors.

Chapter 4: Escaping the Perfection Trap

1 '50% women body shamed at least once in Life: Report', INDIA CSR, 6 April 2019, https://indiacsr.in/50-women-body-shamed-at-least-once-in-life-report/.
2 Seyed Alireza Hosseini and Ranjit K. Padhy, 'Body Image Distortion', 4 September 2023, https://www.ncbi.nlm.nih.gov/books/NBK546582/.
3 Hannah L. Quittkat et al., 'Body Dissatisfaction, Importance of Appearance, and Body Appreciation in Men and Women Over the Lifespan', *Frontiers in Psychiatry* 10, 2019.
4 Kim Parker, Juliana Menasce Horowitz and Renee Stepler, 'On Gender Differences, No Consensus on Nature vs. Nurture: Americans See Different Expectations for Men and Women', Pew Research Center, 5 December 2017.
5 '"Get Real Barbie" Fact Sheet', https://www.chapman.edu/students/health-and-safety/psychological-counseling/_files/eating-disorder-files/13-barbie-facts.pdf.

6 Ibid.
7 Hilary Hurd Anyaso, 'Women No Longer Regarded as Less Competent Than Men but Still Seen as Less Ambitious and Decisive: New Analysis Investigated How Gender Stereotypes Have Evolved Over Seven Decades', Northwestern Now, 18 July 2019.
8 Felicity Menzies, 'Gender Bias at Work: The Assertiveness Double-Bind', LinkedIn, 18 April 2018, https://www.linkedin.com/pulse/gender-bias-work-assertiveness-double-bind-felicity-menzies-fca/.
9 Ibid.
10 SeungYeong Im et al., 'Gender Differences in Aggression-related Responses on EEG and ECG', *Experimental Neurobiology* 27 (6), 2018.
11 'Advancing the Future of Women in Business: The 2022 KPMG Women's Leadership Summit Report', KPMG, 22 January 2022, https://womensleadership.kpmg.us/content/dam/womensleadership/images/2022/kpmg2022_WLS_study.pdf.
12 Jessica Bennett, 'It's Not You, It's Science: How Perfectionism Holds Women Back', TIME, 22 April 2014, https://time.com/70558/its-not-you-its-science-how-perfectionism-holds-women-back/.
13 Brené Brown, 'Perfectionism is Armor: Perfectionism is . . .', LinkedIn, 2019, https://www.linkedin.com/posts/brenebrown_perfectionism-is-armor-perfectionism-is-activity-6422223430090846208-thst/.
14 Gordon L. Flett et al., 'The destructiveness and public health significance of socially prescribed perfectionism: A review, analysis, and conceptual extension', *Clinical Psychology Review* 93, https://hewittlab.sites.olt.ubc.ca/files/2023/01/Flett-Hewitt-et-al-SPP-Destructiveness.pdf.

15 Ayla S. Gelsinger, 'A Critical Analysis of the Body Positive Movement on Instagram: How Does it Really Impact Body Image?', *Spectra Undergraduate Research Journal* 1 (1), digitalscholarship.unlv.edu/spectra/.

16 Jennifer 'Jay' Palumbo, 'The Body Positive Movement Encourages Inclusion, Not Obesity', *Forbes*, 12 May 2022, https://www.forbes.com/sites/jenniferpalumbo/2022/05/12/how-the-body-positive-movement-doesnt-encourage-obesity-but-inclusion/?sh=9bedc1b17371.

Chapter 5: The Guilt Factory

1 Nancy Colier, 'The Guilt That Women Suffer', *Psychology Today*, 12 October 2022, https://www.psychologytoday.com/intl/blog/inviting-monkey-tea/202210/the-guilt-women-suffer.

2 Katarzyna Suwada, 'Parenting, Gender and Work: A Sociological Perspective', *Parenting and Work in Poland: A Gender Studies Perspective*, SpringerBriefs in Sociology (Springer Nature, 2021).

3 Tricia Williamson et al., 'Mothering Ideology: A Qualitative Exploration of Mothers' Perceptions of Navigating Motherhood Pressures and Partner Relationships', *Sex Roles* 88 (2023): 101–117.

4 Brynn Johnson, 'Millennial Moms Are Emotionally Exhausted', *Psychology Today*, 26 May 2021, https://www.psychologytoday.com/us/blog/body-talk/202105/millennial-moms-are-emotionally-exhausted.

5 Caitlin Gibson, 'Millennials are tired of trying to be perfect moms', *Washington Post*, 28 August 2023, https://www.washingtonpost.com/parenting/2023/08/28/millennial-moms-perfection/.

6 Tanja Hentschel et al., 'The Multiple Dimensions of Gender Stereotypes: A Current Look at Men's and Women's Characterizations of Others and Themselves', *Frontiers in Psychology* 10 (2019), https://www.frontiersin.org/articles/10.3389/fpsyg.2019.00011/full.

7 Nancy Colier, 'The Guilt That Women Suffer', *Psychology Today*, 12 October 2022, https://www.psychologytoday.com/intl/blog/inviting-monkey-tea/202210/the-guilt-women-suffer.

8 Ruchira Chakraborty et al., 'Caregiving: a risk factor of poor health and depression among informal caregivers in India - A comparative analysis', *BMC Public Health* 23(1) (2023):42, https://www.ncbi.nlm.nih.gov/pmc/articles/PMC9817300/.

9 Nilanjana Bhowmick, 'I Couldn't Find a Hospital Bed for My COVID-Struck Father in India. Days of Frantic Searching Showed Me How Overwhelmed Our Health System Is', *Business Insider*, 27 April 2021, https://www.businessinsider.in/science/health/news/i-couldnt-find-a-hospital-bed-for-my-covid-struck-father-in-india-days-of-frantic-searching-showed-me-how-overwhelmed-our-health-system-is-/articleshow/82276166.cms.

10 Chie Aoyagi, 'Lessons from Japan: Gender Guilt', International Monetary Fund, 9 September 2020, https://www.imf.org/en/Blogs/Articles/2020/09/09/blog-090920-guilt-gender-lesson-from-japan.

11 Roberta Satow, *Doing the Right Thing: Taking Care of Your Elderly Parents Even If They Didn't Take Care of You* (Los Angeles: Tarcher, 2005).

12 Kelly Hayes, 'Survey: Nearly Half of Americans Admit Talking to Their Plants, and It Might Make Them Happier', Fox 5, 6 September 2022, https://www.fox5dc.com/news/survey-americans-admit-talking-to-plants-might-make-them-happier.

13 Min-Sun Lee et al., 'Interaction with Indoor Plants May Reduce Psychological and Physiological Stress by Suppressing Autonomic Nervous System Activity in Young Adults: A Randomized Crossover Study', *Journal of Physiological Anthropology* 34(1) (2015): 21, https://www.researchgate.net/publication/275666367_Interaction_with_indoor_plants_may_reduce_psychological_and_physiological_stress_by_suppressing_autonomic_nervous_system_activity_in_young_adults_A_randomized_crossover_study.

Chapter 6: The Inheritance of Trauma: Understanding Our Pain

1 Crystal Raypole, 'Understanding Intergenerational Trauma: Effects and Coping Strategies', Healthline, https://www.healthline.com/health/mental-health/intergenerational-trauma, last accessed 10 January 2024.

2 Claire Ryder, 'Women: What We Pass Down', Verve Up, 1 October 2019, https://medium.com/verve-up/women-what-we-pass-down-28e25aaae0b6.

3 Harjyot Kaur and Pooja Jaggi, 'Intergenerational Trauma in the Context of the 1947 India–Pakistan Partition', *Psychological Studies* 68 (2023): 374–87.

4 Udita Iyengar et al., 'Unresolved trauma in mothers: intergenerational effects and the role of reorganization', *Frontiers in Psychology* 5 (2014): 966.

5 Maya Borgueta, 'When It's Not Just Burnout: Recognizing Trauma in the Workplace', Stella Nova, 8 June 2022, https://stellanovawomen.com/workplace-trauma/.

6 'What is Feminism?- Kamla Bhasin's Keynote Speech at the International Seminar Interpreting Feminism vis-à-vis Activism', Sangat Blog, 23 July 2019, https://sangatnetwork.org/2019/07/23/what-is-feminism-speech/.

7 Christina Thomas Dhanaraj, 'I'm a Dalit Woman, and My Mental Health Matters. What We Need Is an Overhaul', *Skin Stories: Essays on Sexuality, Disability and Gender*, Scroll.in, 15 December 2019, https://scroll.in/article/946760/im-a-dalit-woman-and-my-mental-health-matters-what-we-need-is-an-overhaul.

Chapter 7: Mothers and Daughters

1 Karina Margit Erdelyi, 'Can Trauma Be Passed Down From One Generation to the Next?', Psycom, 7 January 2020, https://www.psycom.net/trauma/epigenetics-trauma.

2 Rachel Yehuda, 'How Parents' Trauma Leaves Biological Traces in Children', *Scientific American*, 1 July 2022, https://www.scientificamerican.com/article/how-parents-rsquo-trauma-leaves-biological-traces-in-children/.

3 Mari Grande, 'Understanding The Mother Wound: Signs, Symptoms, and Treatment of Maternal Trauma', LinkedIn, 10 March 2022, https://www.linkedin.com/pulse/understanding-mother-wound-signs-symptoms-treatment-mari/.

4 Bernadette Denise Ward, 'Exploring the Impact of Generational Trauma on Mother-Daughter Relationships with an Emphasis on the African American Community', *Doctoral Dissertations and Projects* 4010 (2022), https://digitalcommons.liberty.edu/doctoral/4010.

5 Karina Margit Erdelyi, 'Can Trauma Be Passed Down From One Generation to the Next?', Psycom, 31 August 2022, https://www.psycom.net/trauma/epigenetics-trauma.

6 Nivida Chandra, 'Were You A "Parentified Child?" What Happens When Children Have to Behave like Adults', *Guardian*, 20 September 2022, https://www.theguardian.com/lifeandstyle/2022/sep/20/parentified-child-behave-like-adult.

Chapter 8: Be the First One on Your To-Do List

1 Kathryn Mayer, 'Gender Pay Gap Has Seen Virtually No Improvement in Two Decades', SHRM, 13 March 2023, https://www.shrm.org/topics-tools/news/benefits-compensation/gender-pay-gap-seen-virtually-no-improvement-two-decades.
2 'Gender Wage Gap in India', Sattva, 19 September 2021, https://www.sattva.co.in/quick-read/gender-wage-gap-in-india/.
3 Rakesh Kochhar, 'The Enduring Grip of the Gender Pay Gap', Pew Research Center, 1 March 2023, https://www.pewresearch.org/social-trends/2023/03/01/the-enduring-grip-of-the-gender-pay-gap/.
4 'New York Life Wealth Watch 2023 Outlook: Individuals Hopeful About Finances, Despite Inflation, Recession Concerns', New York Life, 18 January 2023, https://www.newyorklife.com/newsroom/2023/wealth-watch-2023-hope-despite-inflation-recession.
5 'The Motherhood Penalty', AAUW, https://www.aauw.org/issues/equity/motherhood/.
6 'Empowering Girls & Women', Clinton Global Initiative, United Nations, https://www.un.org/en/ecosoc/phlntrpy/notes/clinton.pdf.
7 Nadya A. Fouad, 'Leaning in, but Getting Pushed Back (and Out)', University of Wisconsin-Milwaukee, August 2014, https://www.apa.org/news/press/releases/2014/08/pushed-back.pdf.
8 Stephanie Watson, 'Forming a Bond With Your Baby -- Why It Isn't Always Immediate', WebMD, 3 October 2022, https://www.webmd.com/parenting/baby/forming-a-bond-with-your-baby-why-it-isnt-always-immediate.
9 Crystal Raypole, 'How to Recognize and Heal from Relationship PTSD', Healthline, 29 April 2021, https://

www.healthline.com/health/relationships/relationship-ptsd.

10 'In India, Women's Self-Help Groups Combat the COVID-19 (Coronavirus) Pandemic', World Bank, 11 April 2020, https://www.worldbank.org/en/news/feature/2020/04/11/women-self-help-groups-combat-covid19-coronavirus-pandemic-india.

11 'Does Gender Inequality Persist Also in Our Leisure Time?', People ACCIONA, 28 July 2022, https://people.acciona.com/diversity-and-inclusion/gender-inequality-leisure/.

12 Mara A. Yerkes, Anne Roeters and Janeen Baxter (2020), 'Gender differences in the quality of leisure: a cross-national comparison', *Community, Work & Family* 23(4), 367–84.